CONTEMPORARY TOPICS IN PARISH LEADERSHIP

Becoming the Good News

A New Approach to Parish Evangelization

Michael J. Sanem

LITURGICAL PRESS

Collegeville, Minnesota

www.litpress.org

Library of Congress Cataloging-in-Publication Data

Names: Sanem, Michael J., author.
Title: Becoming the Good News : a new approach to parish evangelization / Michael J. Sanem.
Description: Collegeville, Minnesota : Liturgical Press, [2023] | Series: Contemporary topics in parish leadership | Includes bibliographical references. | Summary: "In the face of declining religious affiliation, this book offers a more consistent, holistic, and catholic approach to parish evangelization, particularly in the United States"— Provided by publisher.
Identifiers: LCCN 2022042969 (print) | LCCN 2022042970 (ebook) | ISBN 9780814668580 (trade paperback) | ISBN 9780814668597 (epub) | ISBN 9780814668597 (pdf)
Subjects: LCSH: Church renewal—Catholic Church. | Parishes.
Classification: LCC BX1746 .S235 2023 (print) | LCC BX1746 (ebook) | DDC 262/.02—dc23/eng/20221202
LC record available at https://lccn.loc.gov/2022042969
LC ebook record available at https://lccn.loc.gov/2022042970

"Michael Sanem's development of evangelization in *Becoming the Good News* is both compelling and lucid. By filling this book with insights from his years in parish ministry, his theological studies, and his own spiritual growth, Sanem leads us to an appreciation of evangelization as a total parish culture, and not just one more parish program. This is a good book for a pastor to read and a parish council to study."

—Fr. Patrick Rush, pastor emeritus of Visitation Church, Kansas City, Missouri

"Through a first-person account, Michael Sanem will guide you along a journey of faith, gospel and mission. He will open your heart anew to the good news you have received, clarify your vision of the fractured world around you, and show you how to map out a way forward. Invaluable for those in parish ministry, this resource will help every Christian encounter Jesus Christ where he otherwise goes overlooked."

—Paul Turner, pastor of the Cathedral of the Immaculate Conception in Kansas City, Missouri

"Michael J. Sanem has given us a vision of evangelization that is not a recruitment process but a form of physical and spiritual presence. In doing so, he restores a contemplative dimension to evangelization that is often overlooked—those moments when, as he phrases it gracefully, 'Even our silence can evangelize.'"

—Michael Centore, editor of *Today's American Catholic*

"In this one book, Michael Sanem summarizes the history and current culture of evangelization, highlights gifts and dangers within the church and within parish communities and brightens the radical but credible path forward. *Becoming the Good News* should be studied by every parish serious enough about the Gospel to engage in honest, humble self-questioning."

—John Kraus, director of Morning Glory Ministries,
Cathedral of the Immaculate Conception, Kansas City,
Missouri

"In a down-to-earth, readable, and accessible style, Michael Sanem gets at the core mission of discipleship. What does it mean for disciples to be evangelizers? What is involved in the evangelizing mission of the whole people of God? Michael Sanem addresses these thorny issues with insight and wisdom born out of real-life church community experience and engagement. The book challenges our way of thinking about what it means to be church, and the elements involved in its evangelizing mission. Questions for reflection along with added specific thoughts to continue the conversation are components of each chapter, making the book an ideal tool for small group sharing. Take and read. It will change you."

—Biagio Mazza, pastoral associate and director of faith
formation at St. Sabina Parish, Belton, Missouri

*To my parents, John and Sally,
who first nurtured the Good News in me.*

Contents

Part III
Evangelization Is a Radical and Credible Witness to God's Goodness

Introduction:
The Signs of the Times

You've seen the signs of the times. Parishes are closing or combining, Catholic schools are shuttered or merging. Mass attendance and parish membership, on the whole, is declining. Your friends, your kids, your siblings, your parents, maybe even you, have stopped going to Mass. One scandal too far, perhaps, or maybe a long slow drift: one Sunday away turns into a few, then a dozen, then a lifetime. The parish will be lucky to host the funeral.

Generally, religious affiliation is declining in the United States, and the nones, or the nonreligious, are growing. If the nonaffiliated were a single religious denomination, they'd be the largest group in the United States.[1] At the same time, many parish ministry teams, and even entire parishes, are getting older. Young people just aren't lining up to carry the torch for the next generation. If they exist, they are marginal, a small band, maybe a bit more traditional in some sense and a little more radical and eclectic in others. Whether they see themselves as "traditional" or "progressive" Catholics, they remain hard to locate within traditional parish structures and communities. They bounce from parish to parish with ease, as indigent and unbound as Jesus Christ himself.

That said, there are parishes and dioceses bucking these trends, but they are not the norm. Anyone with an unbiased eye on the data, at falling Mass attendance and plummeting religious affiliation, has accepted that simply maintaining the once grand edifice of Catholic Christendom in the United States is no longer a viable strategy. The times are changing.

Enter evangelization initiatives. Perhaps you've also seen them. They adorn the mission statements and visioning documents of most dioceses across the country. They are stapled to every pastoral minister's and faith formation director's long list of to-dos. They manifest as programs, speaker events, parish missions and revivals. They nag at pastors, parish administrators, and parish councils. We scratch our heads and ask: Where is everybody? How can we get them here?

Consider the changes of the past few decades, or even the past few years. We've seen the world order upended. We've experienced a global pandemic that has radically changed how we look at work, family, community, and the social life of our communities. But there are other pandemics: pandemics of fear and violence, pandemics of nihilism and meaninglessness, pandemics of confusion and uncertainty. These pandemics, while not as tragic or deadly as COVID-19, gnaw at the norms and institutions that have given our communal life together a sense of structure, meaning, and purpose. Families are experiencing division, friendships have weakened, and common ground has become difficult to discover. We are awakening to the hard reality that the web of relationships that give our communities stability are growing increasingly more fragile. We are all feeling a bit uprooted.

And yet, as Pope Francis has illustrated in the Preparatory Documents of the Synod on Synodality, the hardships and crises of the past decade have also revealed the deep interconnectedness of all people.[2] A local outbreak becomes a pandemic. A regional conflict inspires a global response. A single tweet becomes a national rallying cry. Small actions, for good and for evil, ripple outward.

This book is also a small action, an attempt to start a conversation about a more consistent, holistic, and Catholic approach to parish evangelization, particularly in the United States. Often our evangelization attempts are hampered by a narrow understanding of our tradition, an all-or-nothing approach to "gaining disciples," and some questionable theological understandings of the church and the world. We look to consultants, to sales strategies, and even to pyramid schemes to create evangelization programs that promise to form missionary disciples, inspire parish renewal, and pack our pews with young, hip, and affluent parishioners.

We can do better.

This book will highlight a very old and, paradoxically, very new, approach to evangelization. It is not an evangelization *program* but a call for our parishes to become an evangelizing *presence* in our communities, in our families, and in the decisions we make as individuals and as churches. It is not consultant-based or guru-driven. There is no monthly fee. It can be implemented at the grassroots level in a way that is organic, life-giving, and focused on the unique gifts, culture, and context of each parish community. It is both decidedly simple and profoundly challenging, because it is nothing less than the gospel call to become witnesses to the incarnate love of God as revealed in the person of Jesus Christ. As such, it invites everyone involved in parish life to be more fully and completely a eucharistic people who, like the disciples on the way to Emmaus, recognize Christ in the "breaking of the bread" and answer the call to become the Mystical Body of Christ in the world, binding up the broken, proclaiming good news to the poor, and affirming and defending the inherent dignity of each and every person.

This approach is based on three principles for parish evangelization: The first is that *everything we do* is a touchpoint of evangelization. This is an invitation to transform our communal life together from within and to examine all the opportunities we have to encounter people in ways that are positive and inspiring. The second principle is that evangelization is discovering the radical goodness of God. This, too, is an invitation for our communities to rediscover who they are in Christ and how Christ invites them—through prayer, service, and the liturgy—into deeper communion and union with God who is Love. And the third principle is that evangelization is a radical and credible witness to God's love for all people. This integrates our understanding of God's goodness into a public witness that can transform our culture. In the chapters ahead, I'll expand on these three principles and invite you to discuss, dialogue, and ask questions of your community in light of them.

When Pope Francis initiated the Synod on Young People in 2018, he said that the purpose of the synod is not to produce documents but "to plant dreams, draw forth prophecies and visions, allow hope to flourish, inspire trust, bind up wounds, weave together relationships, awaken a dawn of hope, learn from one another, and create a bright resourcefulness that will enlighten minds, warm hearts, give strength to our hands."[3] That's my hope for this book as well: to plant a dream of being a church that evangelizes by our presence, by our good works in the world, by the way we welcome, accompany, listen, and encounter people in our communities. In short, it's a dream of a church that seeks ever more to become the good news it proclaims. And I hope that by the end of this book, that might be your dream too.

Part I

Everything We Do Is a Touchpoint of Evangelization

1

A New Moment for the New Evangelization

We must not grow weary of doing the little things for the love of God, who looks not on the great size of the work, but on the love in it.

—*Brother Lawrence*

When I was hired to be the evangelization minister at Church of the Nativity in Leawood, Kansas, a vibrant suburban parish with a growing school and a strong history of committed parishioner engagement in both parish and archdiocesan initiatives, I was tasked with creating an integral vision for evangelization for the parish after I spent some time learning about the culture and charisms of the place and the people there.

The pastor at Nativity is Fr. Mike Hawken, and *"Everything we do is a touchpoint of evangelization"* is one of his favorite phrases. And since I started working here, I've learned it's something he really lives in his interactions with parishioners and visitors. When my uncle died in December of 2021, Nativity hosted the funeral, and Fr. Mike presided at the Mass. My extended family is like yours. There are some very committed Catholics, some "cultural" Christmas and Easter Catholics, some non-Catholics, and a sizable group of former, or disaffiliated Catholics. Some of the latter group drifted away or were scandalized by the abuse crisis or left in anger because of a bad experience. And others were basically forced to leave because of divorce and remarriage, or LGBTQ+ identity, or any number of other hot-button issues.

Fr. Mike presided at the funeral with such gentleness, positivity, and inclusion that every single one of my family members left feeling welcome, appreciated, and invited to return. A Methodist family member said, "Wow, this is the most welcome I've ever felt in a Catholic Church." One of my aunts who has drifted away over the years said, "If I ever come back to the church, it will be because of priests like him." I heard something similar from a coworker who had Fr. Mike preside at her daughter's wedding. All around, he's the kind of priest, person, and pastor that makes you want to be Catholic.

It's clear from his witness and his leadership that he approaches evangelization in a natural, organic, and holistic way. Looking out at a congregation gathered for a funeral or a wedding, Fr. Mike sees both an opportunity to celebrate a beautiful, prayerful liturgy, and an opportunity to share the good news of God's love for each and every person gathered there, no matter who they are, where they come from, or what they believe. There's no fear, there's no coercion, there's just the simple proclamation of the gospel: God reveals who God is in the loving, welcoming witness of Jesus Christ, whom we encounter in the Eucharist and in one another.

"Everything we do is a touchpoint of evangelization" also echoes the ecclesiology of the Second Vatican Council, which points to our witness to the wider world—from worship to social justice to direct service to the poor to dialogue with other religions—as part of evangelization. In this broader understanding, evangelization is not just apologetics, or defending the faith, or some practice of inward-focused spiritual elitism. Instead, it's looking at a world torn by injustice, by violence, by oppression, prayerfully reading "the signs of the times," and then reflecting on how God is calling us to be agents of healing, change, and reconciliation.

It also represents a shift in tone and substance from a lot of evangelization programming I've uncovered. Many evangelization programs look outward at the world with a sense of judgment or pity (or even despair), and then strategize how to "catch" people and convince them of the truth, beauty, and goodness of Catholicism. But this vision rarely leads to any sort of deeper cultural change or prophetic witness that isn't decidedly reactionary or nostalgic. Moreover, these programs are legion, available via a multitude of various Catholic websites, publishers, and consultants. For the right price, you can run an evangelization program at your parish, your school, even your home.

But the genius and challenge of Fr. Mike's vision is that it cannot be enacted by a single person or even a single parish. It requires a shift in both practice and perception of how we look at both evangelization and the relationship between the church, the world, and the culture. And it also forces us to look at ourselves and our communities, to evaluate our own evangelizing presence in the world and the ways we might fall short of living the joy of the gospel.

In many ways, Fr. Mike's "touchpoint" phrase is the genesis of this book. It means that everything we do as a parish—how we welcome people at Sunday Mass, how we answer the phone, how we prepare couples for marriage or a baby for baptism, how we run our capital campaigns, how we treat our staff and volunteers, how we disagree and dialogue with one another—*everything* we do is a potential touchpoint to share the good news with someone. Or, to possibly repel them.

It also asks of us to look beyond the boundaries of our parish, into our homes, neighborhoods, our dioceses, and into the national and global witness of our universal church. And when we do, we discover that for the past several decades, we have had a troubling witness to the wider world, with the clerical sex abuse crisis, church corruption, and constant infighting among prelates and influential Catholics. And especially today, we feel the hurt caused by division and political polarization within our society as it tears at the unity of our communities. Our church, like our culture, has been infected with the pandemics of fear, political division, uncertainty, and meaninglessness.

In the face of this, many popular evangelization initiatives are aimed at a very small group of people and, as such, the net they cast and the size of the catch are small. These approaches often rely on a sort of Catholic doctrinal supremacy, or, as Pope Francis puts it in *Evangelii Gaudium* (The Joy of the Gospel), they are practiced by "those who ultimately trust only in their own powers and feel superior to others because they observe certain rules or remain intransigently faithful to a particular Catholic style from the past." The problem is that this approach, though apparently anchored in "holiness," is incredibly self-centered: "a supposed soundness of doctrine or discipline leads instead to a narcissistic and authoritarian elitism, whereby instead of evangelizing, one analyzes and classifies others, and instead of opening the door to grace, one exhausts his or her energies in inspecting and verifying. In neither case is one really concerned about Jesus Christ or others."[1]

These may seem like harsh words from the Holy Father, but the stakes couldn't be higher: "The mark of Christ, incarnate, crucified and risen, is not present [in these groups]; closed and elite groups are formed, and no effort is made to go forth and seek out those who are distant or the immense multitudes who thirst for Christ."[2] And that's what we are talking about when we speak about everything being a touchpoint of evangelization: the immense multitudes. Without a witness that is holistic, integrated, and authentic, we will never reach the mass of people we hope to engage, inspire, and evangelize.

The Great Opt-Out

As you may have noticed, parish life has changed. People move around a lot more, and the parish is no longer the social center it once was. Maybe you've also noticed that people have stopped coming to church as often as they used to. What once might have seemed controversial, going to Mass one or two times a month, or maybe just a couple times a year, is no longer that exceptional. Even parishes with large and vibrant Catholic schools often find that most school families do not attend Sunday Mass with any sense of regularity. They go when they want, where they want, and to whom they want. It's as if a large number of Catholics, Catholics who might even tithe regularly or pay tuition to the school, have just "opted out" of regular Mass attendance. And these are the ones who still consider themselves Catholic, to say nothing of the vast swathes of disaffiliated that grow a bit larger every day.

What to do in the face of this? The "old school" response would be a heaping helping of hell, a reminder of the gravity of mortal sin, of the binding obligation to go to Mass on Sundays and holy days, and so forth. One missionary priest advised me that the best solution is for the pastor to go to the PTA meeting and say that they were breaking his heart: "Make it personal!" He said, "Rouse up some Catholic guilt, and then people will start coming back to Sunday Mass." But if the guilt approach still worked, we would probably see more Catholics at the confessional each week as well.

Popes Paul VI and John Paul II were prophetic in calling for a "new evangelization," as they certainly saw the signs of the times in Europe, as we are now seeing them in the U.S. But I wonder if even their most dire prophecies could have predicted the wholesale and almost casual "opting out" that many of us are seeing in parish life. The church isn't viewed as the enemy, necessarily, but just irrelevant, inconsequential, and even *useless* in living a fulfilling life. It's as if we are living on a different planet from those we wish to evangelize.

All of this indicates that we are living in a "new moment" for evangelization. Our church has weathered many such moments and often turned crisis into an opportunity to grow in mutual understanding and enlarge our view of God, ourselves, and the saving mission of Christ. Almost from the beginning, an encounter with one of these "new moments" resulted in a mutually enriching process of dialogue, inculturation, and growth in self-understanding for the church and the new followers of Jesus. When St. Paul began to preach the saving love of Christ to the Gentiles, he was met with much resistance. But he persisted and declared something radical for the growing community: "For all of you who were baptized into Christ have clothed yourselves with Christ. There is neither Jew nor Greek, there is neither slave nor free person, there is not male and female; for you are all one in Christ Jesus" (Gal 3:27-28). In that moment, under the guidance of the Holy Spirit, the church itself was enlightened, enlarged, and a vision of God's greater providential action in history was revealed.

Consider also the centuries that followed St. Paul's preaching to the Gentiles: the Christian encounter with Greek philosophy, with the Roman Empire, with Gnosticism and indigenous religions, with the myriad of cultures and languages and traditions that have been touched by the tremendous witness of people who have awakened to God's saving love in Christ, right in the midst of whatever culture, context, or community they find themselves. Reflect upon the gifts of this mutually enriching process of inculturation: the Trinity, the Creeds, our aesthetic history of art, poetry, literature, an enduring (though sometimes baffling) ecclesial structure, a bounty of sacred architecture and systematic theology, Catholic social teaching and a commitment to human rights, social justice, religious freedom, along with a worldwide network of charitable giving and direct aid for those most in need.

Our church is continually called to reflect both charitably and critically on the movements within the culture, and within the life of the church, to carry out our mission more effectively. This is the purpose of the many renewals we've experienced in the life of the church. We are living again in such a moment, when a courageous and authentically Catholic response to the culture is needed. There have been several such responses in the past century, one of which is the calling for a new evangelization, but others, such as the Second Vatican Council, the development of Catholic social teaching, and the call to be a more synodal church, are often missing from typical conversations around evangelization at the parish level. This book aims to remedy that.

All of these changes force us to reckon with the even deeper question: If everything we do is a touchpoint of evangelization, then what is it we, the people of God, the church, are truly called to be doing? What is the mission of the church? And why should we evangelize? And it's to this question that we will turn to in the next chapter.

Questions for Reflection and Discussion

1. Consider all the people who come to Mass each Sunday. In your opinion, what are they looking for? Why do they come? How are they nourished?

2. Consider all the people "missing" from your weekend Masses. Who are they? Why do you think they stopped coming?

3. What is going on in your parish and in your diocese? Are you facing parish and school closings, or growth? How have evangelization initiatives been created, implemented, and received by parish communities?

Continuing the Conversation: Examining Our Motivations

I think it's telling to many that our current conversation around evangelization in the United States is occasioned by a mass exodus of Catholic disaffiliation. In light of this, it can be helpful to examine our motivations for evangelization.

Are we truly distressed by empty pews? Is our desire to grow our parishes based on our love for God or our fear of loss? What is at the heart of our desire for evangelization?

Do we really miss all those young people, those wide swathes of "drifters, dissenters, and injured"? What if they had wounds from their experience of church or from their time away from the church? What if they had hopes and dreams for the church that we weren't quite ready to listen to, let alone accept?

2

The Mission
Has a Church

The church doesn't have a mission; the mission has a church.[1]

At the first Ibero-American Conference of Theology at Boston College, papal delegate Bishop Raúl Biord Castillo of La Guaira, Venezuela remarked, "The church doesn't have a mission; the mission has a church."[2] He went on to state: "When a diocese says, 'What's our mission this year?' that's a reductive concept of mission. Oftentimes we think that a mission is something we have to do, and that's how it's been assumed at various organizations and think groups, etc.—the 'what to do.' Mission isn't even about having more people enter the church. It's about being witness to God's love that includes all people."[3]

That's a great, and succinct, understanding of the church's mission: namely, that the church doesn't have a mission, the mission has a church. And that mission is "being witness to God's love that includes all people." He is also correct in connecting a narrow understanding of the mission with a narrow understanding of evangelization. Because if our sense of mission is too narrow, our understanding of evangelization becomes narrow, and it becomes just another program or committee or "to-do" on our list. For example, if we believe that our mission as Catholics is just to attend Mass each week, be a "good person," and participate in the social life of our parish, we'll miss something essential about the radical nature of the gospel message. Moreover, if we believe our mission is simply to defend the faith from detractors, our evangelization will become strictly apologetic in character, debating and defending without proclaiming anything of real, perennial value.

But, if we look at our mission like Bishop Castillo recommends, in the broad sense, we see a much larger vision of the church being a "witness to God's love that includes all people." With this vision of mission, evangelization becomes the concrete and practical sharing of this love with the world, proclaiming in word and deed the good news of God's incarnate love as revealed to us through the incarnation, life, ministry, teachings, suffering, death, and resurrection of Christ Jesus.

In evangelization ministry, we call this the proclamation of the *kerygma,* the core message of the gospel: salvation experienced in and through Christ Jesus. Perhaps you've seen a few of these. Those signs at football games that read "John 3:16" come to mind: "For God so loved the world that he gave his only Son, so that everyone who believes in him might not perish but might have eternal life." Or Galatians 4:4-7: "But when the fullness of time had come, God sent his Son, born of a woman, born under the law, to ransom those under the law, so that we might receive adoption. As proof that you are children, God sent the spirit of his Son into our hearts, crying out, "Abba, Father!" The early Christians were on *fire* with the *kerygma*; it was their mission to live it and share it, and that *mission*, given by Christ, created the *community*, the church, founded by Christ to continue his mission in the world. That's important to note: the community was created for the sake of the mission, and that's why the community is still being sustained by the Spirit: namely, to fulfill the mission of being a witness to God's love for all people.

In keeping with this received mission, the early Christians welcomed into their midst the uncircumcised and the unclean, the slave and the soldier, the noble and the beggar, the Jew and the Gentile, all in the name of Christ. They impressed and repelled people with their radical witness:

they lived in common, sharing everything and abhorring personal or familial wealth. When plagues arrived in cities, Christians stayed behind to tend to the sick who had been abandoned, often getting sick and dying with those they sought to serve. When persecutions arrived, they were often unreasonably stubborn in their beliefs, embracing death and persecution rather than the "common sense" of the age. In the words of Orthodox theologian David Bentley Hart: "They were rabble. They lightly cast off all their prior loyalties and attachments: religion, empire, nation, tribe, even family. . . . He . . . promised them that in this world they would win only rejection, persecution, tribulation, and failure. Yet he instructed them also to take no thought for the morrow. This was the pattern of life the early Christians believed had been given them by Christ."[4]

Indeed, the early Christians lived more radically than we are even remotely comfortable considering: "The community of believers was of one heart and mind, and no one claimed that any of his possessions was his own, but they had everything in common. . . . There was no needy person among them, for those who owned property or houses would sell them, bring the proceeds of the sale, and put them at the feet of the apostles, and they were distributed to each according to need" (Acts 4:32, 34-35). The animating basis for this radical communal life was the eucharistic understanding they had of themselves, their lives, and their communities. Before the gospels were ever written, before

St. Paul even started preaching, the Christians were baptizing new believers and gathering in their homes to celebrate the Eucharist together. In the breaking of the bread and the breaking open of the Scriptures, they experienced the radical intimacy of the Risen Lord in their gathering, and celebrated together his continued, real presence with them in the Eucharist, in the joy of their community, and in the love they showed to one another.

It's Not About the Numbers

Contrast that picture with the reality of our evangelization initiatives today, which often begin with people in ministry like myself scratching our heads and wondering, "Where did everybody go?" or "Why don't young people come to Mass anymore?" or "What is going to happen to our church if everyone leaves?" I confess that often it's an incredibly fear-based and self-centered approach to changing trends in our culture regarding religious affiliation. One wise pastoral associate once told me, as I complained about the lack of "numbers" in our parish gatherings: "Jesus said feed my sheep, not count my sheep. So if two sheep show up, I'm going to feed them."

Pope Francis shared a similar sentiment in 2022 when he said: "What is the vocation of the Church? It is not numbers. It is to evangelize. The joy of the Church is to evangelize. The real problem is not whether we are few, in short, but whether the Church evangelizes."[5] He was paraphrasing the apostolic exhortation *Evangelii Nuntiandi* (Evangelization in the Modern World) by Pope Paul VI, who wrote that the church "exists in order to evangelize."[6] Similarly, in 2000, the then Cardinal Ratzinger and future Pope Benedict XVI said, "The Church always evangelizes and has never interrupted the path of evangelization. . . . New evangelization cannot mean: immediately attracting the large masses that have distanced themselves from the Church by using new and more refined methods. No—this is not what new evangelization promises. New evangelization means . . . to dare, once again and with the humility of the small grain, to leave up to God the when and how it will grow (Mark 4:26-29)."[7]

Notice the primacy of authentic witness and the integral place of evangelization in the church's mission in the understandings of Popes Paul VI, Benedict XVI, and Francis. They reflect a deep appropriation of *Lumen Gentium* (the Dogmatic Constitution on the Church from the Second Vatican Council), which outlined the basis of the church's self-understanding in the crucifixion of Christ: "The church—that is, the kingdom of Christ already present in mystery—grows visibly in the world through the power of God. The origin and growth of the church . . . were foretold in the words of the Lord referring to his death on the cross: 'And I, if I be lifted up from the earth, will draw all people to myself.'"[8]

So if the church is going to "draw" people to Christ, it should follow the lead of Christ. And did Christ obsess over numbers, budgets, and programs? No, he sought to seek and save, to heal and welcome, to go to the margins, to the lowliest and most rejected, and to touch them, encounter them, heal them, and affirm their worth and dignity. In short, he drew people to himself by being a witness of God's love to all people.

Lumen Gentium affirms this essential link between Christ's witness and our own: "Just as Christ carried out the work of redemption in poverty and oppression, so the church is called to follow the same path if it is to communicate the fruits of salvation to humanity." Time and time again, we have insisted that the church is called to follow Christ in both his message and his *way of living*. *Lumen Gentium* continues: "Christ Jesus, 'though he was by nature God . . . emptied himself, taking the nature of a slave,'. . . and 'being rich, became poor'. . . for our sake. Likewise, the church, although it needs human resources to carry out its mission, is not set up to seek earthly glory, but to proclaim, and this by its own example, humility and self-denial." And how can we evangelize with humility and self-sacrifice? "Christ was sent by the Father 'to bring good news to the poor . . . to heal the broken hearted' . . . 'to seek and to save what was lost.'. . . Similarly, the church encompasses with its love all those who are afflicted by human infirmity and it recognizes in those who are poor and who suffer, the likeness of its poor and suffering founder. It does all in its power to relieve their need and in them it endeavours to serve Christ."[9]

Our mission, therefore, is not just to proclaim the good news but to become the good news, knowing that everything we do is a touchpoint of evangelization. Because everything we do as a parish community is a potential opportunity to share the good news of God's love for all people in Christ. When we serve the world with humility and self-sacrifice, we become authentic witnesses of God's love for the world, of the kingdom of God. Because this authentic witness is the proclamation of the kingdom of God, and "the church . . . is, on earth, the seed and the beginning of that kingdom,"[10] the various structures, hierarchies, ordained ministries, canon law, and indeed, *everything* about the church that has been created, insofar as it is willed by the Spirit, *exists solely for the sake of this mission.*

Going even deeper, we are called to proclaim the radical message that St. Athanasius, a doctor of the church, wrote in the third century: "God became human so that humans could become God."[11] In short, Christ, who is both fully human and fully divine, is the first fruits of what we are called to be. And we are expected to go forth and share this radical reality with a world that suffers from a massive sense of disenchantment, isolation, and the separation from God that we call sin. As Pope Francis has said, "Today the Lord is knocking from within [the church] to be let out,"[12] and as the church, we are called to go forth and "consecrate the world itself to God."[13] Our salvation is not an individual striving, some sort of an afterlife fire insurance policy we purchase by consistent Mass attendance and confession (although they do help). God's mission, which is the reason for our church community's existence, is utterly corporate, communal, and even cosmic. Christ is the "first fruits" of "all creation . . . groaning in birth pangs" (Rom 8:22). In our rest and in our labor, in our living and our dying, we are called to consecrate the world to God, in all its messiness, suffering, and grandeur.

The sacraments, the liturgy, our shared prayer, our understanding and organization of our church and parish communities are all created to witness to that message: "All [people] are called to this union with Christ, who is the light of the world, from whom we come, through whom we live, and towards whom we direct our lives."[14]

Failures of Evangelization

The sad reality, however, is that the church has not always lived in accord with this message. As the *Catechism of the Catholic Church* teaches: "On her pilgrimage, the Church has also experienced the 'discrepancy existing between the message she proclaims and the human weakness of those to whom the Gospel has been entrusted.'"[15] The colonizing history of evangelization, in which we viewed non-Christians (or even non-Catholics) as inferior, or even nonhuman, continues to haunt our conversations on evangelization. We cannot lose sight of the sinfulness of approaches to evangelization that were used to further narratives of slavery, racism, sexism, and elitism. We continue to repent and atone for the human rights abuses and the destruction of peoples and cultures committed in the name of God, Christ, and the church. Indeed, we cannot whitewash the atrocities committed, the peoples enslaved, the cultures destroyed, in the name of evangelization. Far from witnessing to God's saving love for all peoples and the presence of God's grace throughout all the world, our colonial approaches (which in many ways, still continue, albeit with varying levels of militancy) seek to use religion to dominate people and enhance our power, influence, wealth, and status. It's hard to imagine a more anti-gospel message embedded in an evangelization effort.

The *Catechism* acknowledges as much when it says: "Only by taking the 'way of penance and renewal,' the 'narrow way of the cross,' can the People of God extend Christ's reign. For 'just as Christ carried out the work of redemption in poverty and oppression, so the Church is called to follow the same path if she is to communicate the fruits of salvation to men.'"[16]

Pope Francis paraphrases Pope Benedict when pointing to this reality: "Pope Benedict was a prophet of this Church of the future, a Church that will become smaller, lose many privileges, be humbler and more authentic and find energy for what is essential. It will be a Church that is more spiritual, poorer and less political: a Church of the little ones."[17]

We are living this reality in the United States. In the face of a new moment for evangelization, we are tasked with finding the "energy for what is essential" and to become a more humble and authentic witness to Christ's love for all peoples. A "church of the little ones" should not view the culture it finds itself in, whether it be hostile or accommodating, sacred or secular, as the enemy from which it must protect and fortify itself. Instead, a "Church of little ones" seeks to find "God in all things" and create communities in which our witness to Christ's love for us is authentic, and even radical. This approach of looking at everything we do, looking at each and every touchpoint, can renew and transform our parishes from within, drawing on our unique gifts, talents, context and cultures to create a truly catholic approach to evangelization, one that is congruent with the church's saving mission.

In our evangelization efforts, we are called not to be colonizers but consecrators, finding the footprints of God in the people and world that we encounter, drawing it to ourselves through a witness of love, respect, and mutuality. What can be our guide for such an approach?

In the next chapter we will look to our liturgy, especially the Eucharist, the source and summit of our faith, and see how it can inform and become the touchstone of all evangelization efforts.

Questions for Reflection and Discussion

1. "The Church doesn't have a mission. The mission has a Church." Is that your experience of your parish, your diocese, your church? Why or why not?

2. Do the conversations on evangelization at the parish or diocesan level focus primarily on numbers? If so, how can learning that evangelization is *not* about numbers be a helpful way to refocus?

3. The documents of the Second Vatican Council, as well as teachings by Pope Paul VI, John Paul II, Benedict, and Francis all point to the church itself as being called to be "the seed and the beginning" of the kingdom of God. Think of your parish and evangelization in those terms: Is your parish "the seed and the beginning" of the kingdom of God? Does it "witness to God's love" for "all people"? Why or why not?

Continuing the Conversation: Penitential Pilgrimages

In the summer of 2022, Pope Francis made a penitential pilgrimage to Canada, "to a land that has witnessed the martyrdom of indigenous peoples whose children were torn from them at the time of the policies of assimilation and enfranchisement." It was a moving and powerful witness of a church in sincere repentance and the images from the trip continue to stir the soul:

> Tears slowly flowed down their motionless, almost expressionless faces, with gazes fixed on the Pope. In that snapshot—repeated many times during the journey—there is much more than a single life. There is the stifled cry of a people. Men and women who, also because of Catholics, have experienced horrors, and who in that encounter saw themselves recognized, touched, embraced and loved. Tears that expressed chasms, sufferings, hopes before which one can only be silent, open one's arms and welcome. . . . [T]he Pope pointed to a path of reconciliation and healing, as he did in recent months at the Vatican when he received representatives of First Nations, Inuit and Métis indigenous peoples. He initiated a process, a horizon that must be reached, that must be built and nurtured.[18]

In Canada, Pope Francis has blazed a path forward in healing, reconciliation, and evangelization. But, it is only the beginning of a larger process. What "penitential pilgrimages" does your community need to embark upon? To what periphery is your community called to go? Before what "chasms, sufferings, hopes" is our church called to be "silent, open . . . and welcome"?

3

Following the Lead
of Our Liturgy:
Eucharistic Evangelization

No one had earned a place at that supper. All had been invited. . . . His infinite desire to re-establish that communion with us that was and remains his original design, will not be satisfied until every man and woman, from every tribe, tongue, people and nation, shall have eaten his Body and drunk his Blood.

—*Pope Francis,* Desiderio Desideravi[1]

God or Zeus

As a young child, I would often accompany my parents to eucharistic adoration. While I often had some religious picture book with me, I often found myself just sort of sitting there quietly, gazing at the images and artwork of the church or chapel. One particular image still stands out to me: a depiction of the Holy Trinity painted above the altar in a beautiful little stone chapel in Lenexa, Kansas. At one point in the early 1900s, the chapel stood stark and lonely on the frontiers of the Great Plains, surrounded by Kansas farmland and prairies. Today it is dwarfed by the larger modern church and school on the campus, built to accommodate the large suburban sprawl that occurred here in the 1970s and '80s. The strangeness of the image is its very human depiction of God the Father: He sits next to Jesus wearing similar garments to him, but he looks older and a bit thicker, like a placid Zeus or a muscular, tired old Gandalf.

That image of God really stuck with me as a little kid. It was a God that didn't look mean, but he didn't look that nice either. He seemed utterly distant and disinterested, as immobile and unchanging as the stone chapel itself.

So I was surprised, at sometime during my childhood, to hear about the Christian mystics, about people who had had a direct experience of God. I thought this was intensely fascinating, that someone could *know*, or even experience a sense of union with that stern, aloof God that I pictured in mind. But my interest was piqued, and though I loved Mary and the saints (and I still do), the desire for a more direct encounter with God remained in me. As I grew in my faith, I eagerly devoured the writings of any saint or person who could talk about it, such as Augustine, John of the Cross, Teresa of Avila, Thomas Merton, or anyone else who could speak with any sense of clarity about directly encountering God. It seemed at the time the most direct, exciting, and efficient way to do this whole "Catholic Christian" thing.

But I also recognize, in the years of teaching and ministry that have followed, that I'm sort of a weird Catholic. Because for many, the word "mystic" can conjure up images of stained-glass saints and ragged ascetics, or some VIP class of Christian who claims to have exclusive spiritual experiences of God, Christ, or Mary. In spite of this, the twentieth-century theologian Karl Rahner once said, "In the days ahead, you will either be a mystic or nothing at all," meaning that without a lived experience of God's presence, many people would fall away from the faith as cultural Christendom fades and secularism takes hold. And as the twenty-first century unfolds and church disaffiliation grows, I think his insight is proving to be quite prophetic.

As I've grown in my faith and understanding of the Catholic liturgy, however, I've realized that most of our shared prayer and liturgy as Catholics can be viewed as a training ground for mystical experience. The structure of the Mass, the rich sacred symbols, the order of the liturgy, the rosary, eucharistic adoration, all of them create spaces and opportunities for an experience of connection, communion, and union with God and, consequently, with one another. In the sacrament of the Eucharist, we are asked to *eat* and *drink* the Body and Blood, soul and divinity of Christ Jesus. It doesn't get any more explicitly mystical and intimate than that. God desires total union with us, and all our best teachings and liturgical practices point to that reality: "In the Eucharist and in all the sacraments we are guaranteed the possibility of encountering the Lord Jesus and having the power of his Paschal Mystery. The salvific power of the sacrifice of Jesus, his every word, his every gesture, glance, and feeling reaches us through the celebration of the sacraments."[2]

Moreover, the Eucharist points directly to the mission of the church. As Pope Leo the Great wrote, "Our participation in the Body and Blood of Christ has no other end than to make us become that which we eat."[3] The liturgy, especially the Eucharist, points to the union of God with all people as the source and summit of our faith, where all roads lead and from which all grace flows. And what we experience in the liturgy, especially in the Mass and the Eucharist, is beyond words, beyond ideas, beyond concepts, because it is a taste of union with God. It's a sacramental, *mystical* encounter with God in Christ, who gives Godself to us in the Eucharist. An authentically Catholic approach to evangelization will therefore follow the lead of the liturgy we celebrate, the Eucharist we love, and the liturgy in which we discover the God who desires our greatest good.

Following the Lead of Our Liturgy

The document that guides the celebration of the Eucharist is called the General Instruction of the Roman Missal, and at the beginning it states that "[t]he celebration of Mass . . . is the center of the whole of Christian life for the Church both universal and local, as well as for each of the faithful individually. For in it is found the high point both of the action by *which God sanctifies the world in Christ* and of the worship that the human race offers to the Father, adoring him through Christ, the Son of God, in the Holy Spirit."[4] To this end, our liturgy calls for the "conscious, active, and fruitful participation"[5] of everyone who attends Mass, not just the servers or readers or the priest. Because the laity are baptized into the common priesthood of all believers through the grace of baptism, "the whole congregation of the faithful joins with Christ in confessing the great deeds of God and in offering of Sacrifice."[6]

Most Catholics don't think of themselves as sharers in the priestly ministry, and probably for good reason. There have been many different periods in church history, and I believe we might be living in one of them, in which the distinction between the laity and the clergy has been over-emphasized. And although some might welcome a more traditionalist understanding of the ontological difference between the clergy and the laity, you simply can't evangelize the entire world with the witness of only ordained clergy and religious. Indeed, the laity are essential to the church's mission, as clearly articulated in *Lumen Gentium*: "[A]ll Christians in whatever state or walk in life are called to the fullness of christian life and to the perfection of charity, . . . following in his footsteps and conformed to his image, doing the will of God in everything."[7]

"Active and fruitful participation" goes beyond singing the hymns and audibly saying the responses. The laity are called to actively participate in Mass by offering thanks to God (Eucharist means "thanksgiving") and, with the priest, offering Christ to the Father, and with Christ, offering our very selves to God. The oblation we offer with the ministerial priest is therefore both the Body and Blood of Christ and the body and blood of ourselves (we are the mystical Body of Christ, after all). The renowned liturgist Fr. Paul Turner states in *My Sacrifice and Yours*: "At every Mass you put yourself on the altar with the bread and wine. Once they have been transformed into the Body and Blood of Christ, we offer them to the Father together with ourselves."[8]

The glory of this offering, this sacrifice, is that it is given back to us by God, utterly transformed. In the same way that Christ was crucified by human sin, he is returned as the life-giving, resurrected Christ of God. Our offering of the bread and wine will become the Body and Blood of Christ, and we, who offer ourselves, are similarly transformed by the reception of Holy Communion: "There is a direct link between the sacrifice you offer and the Communion you receive . . . when the gifts are brought forward, you are part of the offering to God. You want to be transformed into something even more pleasing to God than you already are. So when you receive Holy Communion, you are sharing in the fruits of the sacrifice you have offered."[9]

This is all echoed in *Lumen Gentium*, which says of the laity: "For all their works, if accomplished in the Spirit, become spiritual sacrifices acceptable to God through Jesus Christ: their prayers and apostolic undertakings, family and married life, daily work, relaxation of mind and body, even the hardships of life if patiently borne. . . . In the celebration of the Eucharist, these are offered to the Father in all piety along with the body of the Lord. And so, worshipping everywhere by their holy actions, *the laity consecrate the world itself to God.*"[10]

Called to Consecrate the World to God

Let me repeat that: "The laity consecrate the world itself to God." It's part of our mission as members of the priesthood of all the baptized. As the ministerial priest offers bread and wine on the altar, so we, too, offer our very lives, our sacrifices, our struggles, our gifts, and all that we encounter, on that same altar. This is our mission!

In a speech to the Pontifical Liturgical Institute in May 2022 in Rome, Pope Francis further articulates this connection between liturgy and mission, underlining three particular dimensions. The first is the "active and fruitful participation in the liturgy." He states that it is necessary "to be imbued with the spirit of the liturgy, to feel its mystery, with an ever-new wonder. The liturgy cannot be possessed, no; it is not a profession: the liturgy is learned, the liturgy is celebrated."[11] In our active participation in the liturgy, we are humbled by God's presence with us, in the Word and in the Eucharist, but we are also formed in a particular way as we enter more deeply into the spirit of it.

The second dimension of liturgy and mission Pope Francis highlights is the "ecclesial communion inspired by the celebration of the Eucharists and the Sacraments of the Church." This eucharistic understanding also serves as the basis for unity as a church: "the liturgical life opens us up to the other, to the nearest and farthest from the Church, in common belonging to Christ." Put quite simply, the liturgy should bring us all together. We see our neighbors, those we agree with and those we don't, those who regularly attend and those who don't, trying their best to be present, to live a good Christian life, and we find our unity in the offering up of ourselves on the altar. It is this decidedly experiential, physical, and non-ideological way of being together in the liturgy that forms the basis for unity and charity toward one another. Pope Francis continues: "Rendering glory to God in the liturgy finds its counterpart in the love of neighbor, in the commitment to living as brothers and sisters in everyday situations, in the community in which we find ourselves, with its merits and its limitations. This is the road of true sanctification."[12]

Liturgy leads us to true sanctification because it helps us grow, little by little, in love of God and love of neighbor, fulfilling the greatest commandment of Jesus. And the nourishment, love, awe, and wonder we experience in the liturgy sends us out into the world, on mission. Here it is helpful to remember that the term "Mass" comes from *missa*, which means "dismissed" or "sent." In the words of Pope Francis: "Every liturgical celebration always concludes with the mission." We are nourished by the Eucharist to become a eucharistic people sent out into the world, to "encounter the world that surrounds us, to encounter the joys and the needs of many who perhaps live without knowing the gift of God."[13] We move toward and flow forth from the liturgy: it calls us to offer our very selves and sacrifices, to bind us together into community, and to send us forth into the world.

The third dimension that Pope Francis highlights is "the impetus to the evangelizing mission, starting out from the liturgical life that involves all baptized persons."[14] The liturgy draws us together, it binds us to one another, and to God in Christ. We bring forward our oblations, our offerings of our lives and the sacrifices we've made for our family, our children, our friends, and people in need out in the world. These humble offerings are consecrated and offered by the ministerial priest in union with the priesthood of all the baptized to God, who generously returns them to us as the nourishment we need to continue being the eucharistic people out in the world: the church, the people of God, the sign and sacrament of God's healing presence, and "the seed and the beginning" of God's kingdom in the swirling tides of history.

As it relates to evangelization, we have to remember, as Pope Francis teaches, that the "genuine liturgical life, especially the Eucharist, always impels us to charity, which is above all openness and attention to others. This attitude always begins and is founded in prayer, especially liturgical prayer. And this dimension also opens us up to dialogue, to encounter, to the ecumenical spirit, to acceptance."[15] Far too often I have heard from would-be Catholic evangelizers, "We have the Eucharist!" as if it were a weapon or a treasure that we have to keep to ourselves, hoarding it behind privacy fences and membership fees lest we lose it. We don't "have" the Eucharist, the Eucharist "has" us, and it impels us to meet people out in the world with sincere charity and hearts open to peaceful dialogue and genuine encounter.

The Sacramental Imagination

The liturgy also forms us in other more subtle ways. I remember one Sunday afternoon, a few hours after Mass, I was helping set the table for a dinner for my extended family. As I was pouring the rich red Brunello into the glasses, the thought just popped into my head: this is holy, this is sacred. Pouring the wine, slicing the bread, placing the plates, pulling up the chairs, all of it suddenly became liturgical, sacred, even sacramental. My Sunday dinner was the mirror of the Sunday Mass, and the Sunday Mass is the mirror—the doorway—into the never-ending feast to come.

I've experienced the same while caring for my children, rocking them to sleep or reading with them, giving them a bath or just noticing the way the light shines through their eyes. I write extensively about it at my website, Incarnation is Everywhere.[16] *Incarnation is everywhere* isn't an ideology, it's an experience, the experience I've been having since I was a child sitting at Mass: "The liturgy is done with things that are the exact opposite of spiritual abstractions: bread, wine, oil, water . . . The whole of creation is a manifestation of the love of God, and from when that same love was manifested in its fullness in the cross of Jesus, all creation was drawn toward it."[17]

The liturgy teaches us that our life of faith together is thoroughly permeated by the presence of God by way of tangible things. It's thoroughly sacramental. The statues and sacred vessels, the dappled light of the stained glass, the smell and sight of incense rising, the feel of the holy oil in your hands, the delightfully medieval musk of chrism upon a baby's brow, the rich and colorful vestments of presider and server, the sacred art and architecture wrapping us all in God's embrace: it all points to God mediated in and through all things. As we consume the Eucharist, God lives in us, and as we sit in our sacred space, surrounded by a community of believers, we also live in God. This is the mystery of the liturgy in which we are formed, as Pope Francis articulates: "The Church today, as always, needs to live the liturgy. . . . We must continue this task of being *formed by* the liturgy. The Blessed Virgin Mary, together with the Apostles, prayed, broke the Bread and lived charity with everyone. Through their intercession, may the liturgy of the Church make present, today and always, this model of Christian life."[18]

And if you enter deeply into our liturgies, into our God-soaked faith, it's a bit easier to discover a God-soaked world, and even a God-permeated universe, or cosmos. That's the sacramental imagination that our liturgy forms us in, the "ever ancient, ever new" offered by the sacramental and liturgical experience of being Catholic. The Real Presence of Christ encountered in the Eucharist ripples outward, so we begin to see Christ also at work in the liturgy itself, in the Word of God, in the presider, in the community gathered and sent forth on mission. Christ is living and active in the world, consecrating the world itself to God.

But how are we to go about doing this in our contemporary world? How can we "become the good news" and be an evangelizing presence in our families, communities, cities, and country? Who can help us connect the experience of the Mass with the impetus toward our mission? The next chapter will point to Mary, Mother of the Church, the Star of the New Evangelization, and highlight her relational, incarnational, Christ-centered method of evangelization.

Questions for Reflection and Discussion

1. "Ours is a God-soaked faith." Is your experience of your parish, and your prayer life together, "God-soaked"? Is there a sense of mystery, of reverence, of awe and wonder in your liturgical life together?

2. Do your evangelization initiatives, either at a parish or diocesan level, connect with the liturgy? Is the Eucharist the "source and summit" of your evangelization? Why or why not?

3. Does the liturgy and shared prayer inspire a sense of being sent on mission, of going forth into the community, into our neighborhoods, into our homes?

Continuing the Conversation:
You Are What You Eat

"Leo the Great writes, 'Our participation in the Body and Blood of Christ has no other end than to make us become that which we eat.'"[19]

One priest once told me, "The reason people don't believe in the Real Presence of Christ in the Eucharist is because when they encounter us, they don't experience people who have been transformed by it."

Is your parish, and are your parishioners, becoming the Christ they eat? What are signs of this in your community? How would an outsider know you are a people transformed by the Real Presence of Christ?

4

Following the Lead of Our Lady: Incarnational Evangelization

Star of the new evangelization,
help us to bear radiant witness to communion,
service, ardent and generous faith,
justice and love of the poor,
that the joy of the Gospel
may reach to the ends of the earth,
illuminating even the fringes of our world.

—Pope Francis, Evangelii Gaudium[1]

Following the Lead of Our Lady

My favorite title for Mary is Madonna della Strada, or Our Lady of the Way (or even Our Lady of the

Highway). This was St. Ignatius of Loyola's favorite as well, as he always wanted his Jesuits to be on the move. So when I started a job in the evangelization ministry, I was eager to ask Mary, Our Lady of the Way, to pray for me. I was new to this type of ministry and was not entirely comfortable with it.

Providentially, within my first few months of my new job I was introduced to Fr. Peter Marsalek, general priest servant for the Society of Our Lady of the Most Holy Trinity, who was working on an evangelization program called DISCIPLE. Following the charism of his order, the approach is very trinitarian, very Marian, and is steeped in the documents of the Second Vatican Council and the writings of Popes John Paul II, Benedict, and Francis.

One time, before a talk on evangelization, Fr. Peter related to me that he had a few minutes to come up with a catchy way to connect Our Lady of Guadalupe with evangelization. He thought of an acronym: R.I.C.E., which stands for Relational, Inculturated, Christ-centered, and Ecclesial. It brilliantly connects our understanding of Mary, discipleship, and evangelization. Below, I'll quote directly from his teaching and then offer my own perspective.

1. Mary's Evangelization Is Relational

"In Mary's words, we see the tenderness of a mother. By establishing her maternal relationship with Juan Diego, she creates an atmosphere of trust and confidence. In a similar way, we too are reminded that the best kind of evangelization occurs with people to whom we have a relationship."[2]

Our Lady of Guadalupe reminded Juan Diego that she is his mother, and a loving mother, at that: "I am your merciful mother, to you, and to all the inhabitants on this land." She lets him know that she knows and loves him, deeply, that they have a relationship, and that relationship is important to her. She also establishes a maternal relationship with everyone else in the Americas in their encounter. In the same way, in our evangelization efforts, we need to put in the work of being in relationship with people, not solely for the sake of evangelizing, but for the sake of the person and the gift of community. This is where "becoming the good news" enables us to be free from coercive methodologies or pretending to be something we are not. We are free in Christ to be who we truly are and let others be who they truly are. We can leave the rest to the Holy Spirit, to God in Christ, and the intercession of our Blessed Mother and the saints.

I think we can even go further with this idea and challenge ourselves and our parish communities to enter into dialogue with people of different faiths, perspectives, cultures, and communities—in short, not to form relationships for the sake of evangelization, but to form relationships for the sake of the relationships. Like Christ, we are invited to enter freely into an authentic encounter with another and to discover how God may already be at work in their lives.

2. Mary's Evangelization Is Inculturated

"Mary came dressed as an Aztec, her appearance was replete with understandable and powerful symbols that the Aztecs understood. She shared the truth of the gospel in a manner that the local people could understand and appreciate. We are called to present the truth of Christ in a manner and language which people can understand."[3]

One strange thing about Mary's apparitions is that, in an incredibly beautiful act of incarnational evangelization, she changes her appearance and the miraculous signs of that appearance depending on whom she is talking to. To St. Bernadette, a young French girl, she appears as a young French girl, incredibly beautiful, and speaking Bernadette's language in a way that she can understand. Yet she is also careful enough to speak to the ecclesial hierarchy, through Bernadette, in a language they can understand, calling herself the Immaculate Conception. In Fatima, Mary speaks the language of the children and even appeals to their need for a miraculous sign (which, incidentally, she does in all three of these accounts), making the sun dance for a large crowd of pilgrims.

And in Guadalupe, Mary becomes even more visibility inculturated to Juan Diego and the people of Mexico. She appears with the brown skin of an indigenous Mexican, not with the whiter complexion of the European apparitions. She speaks to Juan Diego in Nahuatl, his native language, and, on the tilma that still holds her image, she incorporates symbols from Aztec religion: the rays of the sun behind her would be recognized as a sign of the sun god Huitzilo-pochtli, and the moon at her feet connects with both the moon god of darkness and the Aztec word from Mexico, "Metz-xic-co," which literally means "in the middle of the moon." Her clothes are filled with meaningful symbols: the black ribbon around her waist shows that she is pregnant, and the four petaled jasmine over her stomach indicates the presence of the Aztecs' highest deity, Ometeotl. Even the flowers on her dress represent hills and rivers, both considered privileged places of encounter between God and humanity to the indigenous people. There are even more symbols to discover, but all point to the radical reality that Mary becomes inculturated to the people to whom she appears, clothing herself in their skin, symbols, and clothes. Like Christ, she becomes "incarnate" in the culture she is evangelizing. It's a powerful message from our Blessed Mother that we must respect the diversity of cultures and be not just respectful, but even incarnational and appreciative, in our approach to them.

3. Mary's Evangelization Is Christocentric

"Mary comes with Jesus, pointing to Him as being true God and Savior. Similarly, our evangelization efforts are called to be centered on the person of Jesus Christ."[4]

Mary follows the lead of Christ, emptying herself and becoming "incarnate" in the culture in which she is appearing. She establishes a close, loving, maternal relationship with Juan Diego, a relationship that isn't dependent upon any particular outcome. This creates trust. But she also doesn't point to herself, she points to Christ. She "becomes the good news" of Christ's saving mission. It is no longer she that lives, but Christ that lives in her.

Why is this important? It's because salvation is not a spectator sport. We are saved through Christ, who assumed our human nature, who restores to us our original belovedness in God, and who invites us deeper and deeper into the divine life. Through him, we become fully united to God in Christ, coheirs to the salvation of God. No one else can offer this to us, and it's why we need to point continually to the person of Christ, and imitate his solidarity with us, in our evangelization efforts.

4. Mary's Evangelization Is Ecclesial

"Mary patiently chose to work through the local bishop, despite the fact that it took multiple visits, and even a few miraculous signs. It is always helpful that our work be connected and rooted in the life of the Church and that it be directed toward bringing others to the Church, the instrument of the ministry of Jesus in the world today."[5]

It sometimes appears that evangelization would be easier if we could bring Christ to people without the messiness of the institutional church. But as we discussed in a previous chapter, the church is continually called to be more and more a sign and sacrament of God's saving mission in the world. Mary chooses to connect the salvific love of Christ with the local, visible church. That means *your* church, your parish, and your diocese, in all its messiness, all its ordinariness, all its unglamourous routine. Following Mary's lead, our evangelization efforts should always point toward our parishes and local church communities. Parishes offer stability and an opportunity for intergenerational dialogue. They create and form community and community-oriented people. They evangelize their communities through a culture of care and concern, and at their best, they are a school of love with an abundant diversity of peoples, languages, and cultures, gathered together to grow deeper in love with Christ and God's people.

I am saddened and troubled by the division in the church today, particularly in the United States. There is a fairly vocal "American schism" taking place, with widespread and open denigration of Pope Francis. There are those who quite openly seek to "purge" the church of any Catholic that does not share their same cultural, political, and spiritual convictions. But in Christ, we are called to even deeper communion, with God, with one another, with nature, and indeed, with all of creation. We are called to union with the Word made Flesh, through which all things are made, and in whom all things live and move and have their being. And we are called to be a visible sign of that love to all the world, a city on a hill, a lamp set on a lampstand, a light to the world. We need community, we need the church, and we need one another to live out the vocation given us by Christ. No person, or parish, is an island; we belong to one another.

The RICE model of evangelization shows us the way Our Lady evangelizes. It also illustrates that evangelization happens in *relationship*, and that evangelization respects different cultures and inculturates the faith within those cultures, creating diverse expressions. Evangelization should always point to and center upon Christ, and evangelization comes from and moves toward the greater church community.

Questions for Reflection and Discussion

1. Reflect on the RICE model of evangelization: How is your parish already evangelizing in ways that are relational, inculturated, Christ-centered, and ecclesial? How could you grow in these?

2. What are the places of division within your parish? Are they cultural, political, social, economic? How are conflicts and divisions dealt with? How could synodality, or walking together, help delineate and reconcile these divisions?[26]

Continuing the Conversation: Touchpoints

What are the touchpoints in your parish? What encounters with parishioners, visitors, guests, and community members are touchpoints of evangelization? Consider what parish programs you invest in and whom they serve.

Think of all the places your parish community encounters one another and encounters guests and visitors: Sunday Mass, daily Mass, weddings, funerals, marriage preparation, baptism preparation, religious education and/or a parish school, ministries of care, RCIA, Bible studies, Knights of Columbus, small faith groups, outreach to the larger community, signage on the property, and so forth.

In each of these contexts, are the pastor, the staff, the volunteers aware of these many touchpoints of evangelization? Is there an intentional effort to be a hospitable, welcoming presence?

Part II

Evangelization Is Getting to Know the Radical Goodness of God

5

The God of
the Good News

*Nothing is more practical than finding God, that is fall-
ing in love in a quite absolute, final way.*

—Pedro Arrupe, SJ

Hellvangelization

If you ever drive across I-70 in my home state of Missouri,
you will encounter a plethora of garish billboards that
often detract from the natural cliffs and hills and general
Ozarkian beauty of the Show-Me State. But sprinkled
among the advertisements for auto stores, fast food, real
estate agents, and "showtime clubs," you will also find some
rather strange attempts at evangelization:

"WHERE ARE YOU GOING? HEAVEN OR HELL."

"ARE YOU READY TO MEET JESUS?" with a flatlining EKG next to it.

And my personal favorite: "HELL IS REAL."

I call this "hellvangelization." It's an effort to evangelize, or spread the good news, by using fear, dread, or hell as the starting point for the conversation about the all-loving, self-emptying, incarnate God that has been revealed in the person of Jesus Christ. For certain people, it might seem appropriate and even effective. We might be tempted to think, if the honey of God's everlasting love doesn't work, how about a little bit of the burning vinegar of God's everlasting wrath? And hellvangelization's power to control and influence people (and even entire populations), is well attested-to in the long history of Christendom.

But in today's culture, there are more than a few problems with this approach. One, I imagine that not many people, particularly young people in the United States, are swayed by this method. There simply isn't enough of a widespread belief in the reality of sin or even God to generate enough social pressure to inspire wholesale repentance using hell as a starting point. In short, there are too many popular alternatives. For example, if you had to choose between an eternity in hell and, say, atheism, which would you choose? It appears that most disaffiliated people are choosing the latter.

Even if hellvangelization worked, what kind of disciples would it create? If someone converts to Christianity due to fear and self-interest, then chances are that they will be fearful and self-interested Christians. Are these the type of disciples Jesus cultivated?

Moreover, the data on mental illness in the United States shows an alarming rise in depression and anxiety in both young people and adults, with nearly one in five adults struggling with depression or anxiety, and 15 percent of young people having experienced a major depressive episode.[1] If you are struggling with intense anxiety or major depression, when daily routines can become difficult and even impossible to perform, then your life might already feel like hell, and every day could be a struggle for survival. In this context, hellvangelization isn't just ineffective, it's abusive. It projects the depression and hopelessness of the present moment onto God and onto eternity. In this context, atheism, scientism, and secularism can appear like a soothing balm, a coherent way of seeing the world, and a healthy alternative to believing in a God who creates us with persistent patterns of mental and physical illness and then punishes us for having them.

Hellvangelization also doesn't at all follow the example of Christ and the early apostles. Look at Paul's letters or the creeds of the early church, and nowhere will you find an eternal hell as the impetus for evangelization or belief in God in Christ. All that you will find is a mention that Christ "descends into hell (or Hades, the realm of the dead)," after his crucifixion for the sake of *saving* the souls that were there. Following the lead of Jesus, we, too, are called to harrow hell and not simply to terrify people with the threat of it.

It's also a decidedly coercive method of evangelization that inspires a selfish discipleship. Imagine if Jesus told the rich young man: "Sell what you have and give your money to the poor. Then, come follow me. If you don't I will torture you for eternity." Add that same message to the calling of Peter and James, to Nathaniel under the fig tree, to Matthew in the tax collector's booth, to Mary Magdalene, to the Samaritan woman. Suddenly the Christ who came so that "they might have life and have it abundantly" strips his disciples of dignity and freedom. "Be not afraid" suddenly becomes "Be very afraid."

Put quite simply, the portrait that hellvangelization paints of God, Father, Son, and Holy Spirit, is utterly horrid. How can anyone get to know the radical goodness of God through a hellvangelizing witness? Add in an unhealthy dose of substitutionary atonement understanding of salvation (in which Jesus's crucifixion is God's wrath toward us poured on an innocent victim, or Jesus as a substitute for our sins, appeasing a bloodthirsty God), and you get a perverse and distorted version of the gospel message, more in line with the very worst strands of Reformed theology than anything that could remotely be called Catholic or Orthodox.

The saving mission of Christ, revealed in his incarnation, ministry, passion, death, and resurrection was understood by the evangelists and St. Paul and all the early Christians as a great overthrowing of the evil powers of sin and death, the "powers and principalities" that govern the cosmos and cause untold suffering for the human person and all creation. Christ, the "image of the invisible God, the firstborn of all creation," destroyed the diabolical power that sin and death had over us by offering his very life: "obliterating the bond against us, with its legal claims, which was opposed to us, he also removed it from our midst, nailing it to the cross; despoiling the principalities and the powers, he made a public spectacle of them, leading them away in triumph by it" (Col 2:13-15). The mission of Jesus the Christ, the Anointed One of God, is salvific not because it saves us from an angry God (which is not only a logical absurdity given the doctrine of the Trinity, but indeed is a horrid thing to imagine) but quite the opposite: it saves us by drawing us into union with God in Christ.

That is good news, for a world torn by violent division, pandemic, and social turmoil, and for all those people suffering in abject poverty or from mental illness, for people in deep despair or nihilism, to those struggling with divorce, rejection, or the myriad of hardships this life heaps upon us and those we love. *Emmanuel, God-with-us, is with you.* And the God of the good news is truly good. In Jesus's words, this God is like a loving father or mother. Not a despot, not a tyrant, there were plenty of those in Jesus's day as there are in ours. No, Jesus insists that God is *abba*, an utterly loving, close, and intimate father who gives good things to those who ask.

God Is the True, the Good, and the Beautiful

The *Catechism of the Catholic Church* states without qualification that God is Love and God is Truth:

> God, "He who is," revealed himself to Israel as the one "abounding in steadfast love and faithfulness" [Exod 34:6]. These two terms express summarily the riches of the divine name. In all his works God displays not only his kindness, goodness, grace, and steadfast love, but also his trustworthiness, constancy, faithfulness, and truth. "I give thanks to your name for your steadfast love and your faithfulness" [Ps 138:2; cf. Ps 85:11]. He is the Truth, for "God is light and in him there is no darkness"; "God is love," as the apostle John teaches [1 John 1:5; 4:8].[2]

And yet, I find among many people, especially among many would-be Catholic evangelizers, a view of God that is decidedly dark, even diabolical. There are a multitude of possible reasons for this. Psychologically, many of us might still carry an image of God we formed in childhood. So if we had a vindictive father or an aloof mother, we might associate that same moodiness or violence to God, which, in turn, we may imitate or even glorify as we raise our own children and attempt to grow in our faith.

Theologically, many of us are accustomed to thinking of God as the Supreme Being *within creation*, who is *out there* or *over there* or *ruling over us* from a distant heaven. This is the God that materialists and atheists have said does not "exist," because there is no evidence of a "god particle" or "god-like being" within the created order. We look for God through a telescope or microscope and cannot find any material evidence of divinity. Sadly, many Catholics and Christians have absorbed this view, that God is another *thing* within the created world, like the sun or the stars or the galaxy. Some may have even absorbed the Enlightenment view of Deism, which believes God created the universe like a clockmaker creates a clock: he designs it with intense craftsmanship and dedication, and then he departs from it, letting creation "run" without God being present to it.

But all of these views represent a category error. God is not another thing within creation, but the ground of all creation itself. God is not another *being*, but the font of all Being, Being itself. God does not *exist* like anything else exists, because God is the source and goal and fullness of existence itself. God, who revealed Godself to Moses in the burning bush, is the One, the only one in fact, who proclaims, "I AM WHO AM," and who is utterly noncontingent and unconditioned. God is "holy," "other," set apart because no-thing is like God, because God isn't just a good, true, and beautiful being. Instead, God is the Good, the True, and the Beautiful, and all created things reflect and participate in this: "All creatures bear a certain resemblance to God, most especially [humankind], created in the image and likeness of God. The manifold perfections of creatures—their truth, their goodness, their beauty—all reflect the infinite perfection of God. Consequently we can name God by taking his creatures' perfections as our starting point, 'for from the greatness and beauty of created things comes a corresponding perception of their Creator.'"[3]

Those traits of truth, goodness, and beauty, those "manifold perfections of creatures," are called the "transcendentals" in Catholic theology and philosophy. Put quite simply, they mean that God is not simply a "good" being or a good "thing," but instead, that God is the source of all goodness; God is goodness itself. God is not another "beautiful" being or thing in creation, or even the most beautiful thing in all creation, but instead, God is Beauty itself, in which all beautiful creatures participate. When we creatures are good, true, and beautiful, we participate in the very nature of God. And all things swirling around us that are good, true, and beautiful, all creation dancing the cosmic dance of moonrise and sunset and starshine, point to the ultimate perfection of the fully transcendent God by whom all things were made.

This view of God in philosophy and theology is called classical theism, or the classical theist tradition, and it is a rich, multicultural tradition that spans millennia and religious traditions with ease and flexibility. Indeed, it is one of the great hallmarks of this tradition that it found brilliant adherents in the great thinkers of Greek philosophy, namely, Plato, Aristotle, and Plotinius, in Jewish philosophers such as Philo of Alexandria and Maimonides, in such brilliant Muslim thinkers and philosophers as Al-Kindi, Al-Farabi, Ibn Sina, and Averroes, and firm adherents within Catholic Christian and Orthodox tradition, such as St. Augustine, St. Gregory of Nyssa, St. Maximus the Confessor, St. Clement of Alexandria, St. Basil of Caesarea, St. Cyril of Alexandria, St. John Damascene, Pseudo-Dionysius, St. Anselm of Canterbury, and St. Thomas Aquinas.

So the God of the good news, the God of classical theism, the God who is the ground of all being, who is the source and end of all creation and utterly immanent to all creatures, in whom we "live and move and have our being," whom we see most clearly reflected in the transcendentals of the Good, the True, and the Beautiful and, most clearly, as agapic and charitable love, is not a construction of some New Age or postmodern spiritual sensibility. Rather, it is well within Catholic Christian Orthodoxy and the depths of our Catholic intellectual tradition, addressed in both the Hebrew Scriptures and New Testament, continually challenging us to grow in our awareness of God in the world, affirming God's immanence as well as divine transcendence.

This is especially important to remember when we consider the concept of "truth" as it relates to evangelization. When we Catholics talk about the ultimate truth, we often point to our catechism or our tradition, maybe our sacraments, or possibly Scripture. And Catholics of particular political persuasions may point to one or two doctrines as the most important part of our faith, the "true" truth that we need to focus all our attention on. But in fact, the Catholic view is that the fullest and ultimate expression of truth is not a doctrine or even a dogma, but instead, is God, to whom all our teachings and traditions point. Even the *Catechism* is careful *not* to box God or even truth into a single definition: "God transcends all creatures. We must therefore continually purify our language of everything in it that is limited, image-bound or imperfect, if we are not to confuse our image of God—'the inexpressible, the incomprehensible, the invisible, the ungraspable'—with our human representations. Our human words always fall short of the mystery of God."[4]

How, then, can we best approach this mystery? How can we, in our evangelizing, discover the radical goodness of God? The answer, of course, is prayer. We discover God's goodness by being in relationship with God and discovering God in the love of that relationship. It is to this, to prayer and contemplative evangelization, which teaches us about the goodness of God, that we will turn next.

Questions for Reflection and Discussion

1. What is your operative image of God? What do you think is the operative image of God in your parish, in your family, in your communities? What image of God did you grow up with and how has it changed?

2. How do fear, coercion, and manipulation enter into your conversations about evangelization? How prominent is "hellvangelization" within your community?

Continuing the Conversation: Your Parish Transcendentals

Classical theism points to the reality that God is the True, the Good, the Beautiful. The gospel teaches us that God is Love.

Where and how does your parish provide opportunities for people to experience the Good, the True, and the Beautiful? How about the reality that God is Love? How could you create experiences and opportunities, both within the liturgy and outside of it, for people to experience the God who deeply loves them?

6

Contemplative Evangelization: Finding God in Prayer

God became human so that humans could become God.

—St. Athanasius

Consequently those who by faith are spiritual members of Christ can truly say that they are what he is: the Son of God and God himself.

—Blessed Isaac of Stella

God's Radical Love

The radicality of the Christian message, the reason for our evangelization, is that the God of the transcendentals, the God who is revealed in ultimate goodness, beauty, truth, and love, became incarnate in Christ in a witness of God's radical love for all people. If we believe in the incarnation of God in Christ, we believe that God emptied Godself to become human: "God became human so that humans could become God," in the words of St. Athanasius. Or as St. Gregory Nazianzus wrote: "What has not been assumed has not been redeemed"[1]—meaning that God had to become *fully human* in Christ to *fully heal* our humanity. This overflowing goodness of God invites us into ever deeper life and identification with Christ, as St. Gregory wrote: "Let us seek to be like Christ, because Christ also became like us: to become gods through him since he himself, through us, became a man. He took the worst upon himself to make us a gift of the best."[2]

This is the great movement of incarnation and redemption: God enters into creation and "makes his dwelling among the human race." The God of overflowing love goes even further, continuing his self-emptying, being born in a stable, as a poor person among the very poor, living among them and teaching, healing, and binding people and communities back together again. He's received warmly by those with nothing and soon gathers a following of misfits, rabble, and "sinners" as disciples. Aside from a few outliers, the wealthy and religious leaders completely reject him and seek instead to trap and destroy him. Jesus, in the face of this, practices complete solidarity with all those thought to be outside the boundaries of God's favor, to the point of dying as a crucified criminal in utter desolation on the cross: The incarnate God tortured and hung on a tree, wholly rejected by those with power and dominion in this world.

But the story doesn't end there, and that's the good news. The apparent destruction of the Living One is transformed into our salvation. Nothing, not even death, will stop the God of Love who seeks to be fully reconciled with all creation.

In the decades following the resurrection, the disciples and apostles would reflect even more deeply on who Jesus was, how Jesus saves us, and how Jesus reveals the face of God to us. One such reflection is found in the Gospel of John, where we see that this Jesus, now recognized as the Christ, was one in being with God, as the Word, or *Logos:*

> *In the beginning was the Word,*
> *and the Word was with God,*
> *and the Word was God.*
> *He was in the beginning with God.*
> *All things came to be through him,*
> *and without him nothing came to be.*
> *What came to be through him was life,*
> *and this life was the light of the human race;*
> *the light shines in the darkness,*
> *and the darkness has not overcome it. (John 1:1-5)*

The word "Word" or "Logos" is a combination of three different cultural understandings: "God's dynamic, creative word (Genesis), personified preexistent Wisdom as the instrument of God's creative activity (Proverbs), and the ultimate intelligibility of reality (Hellenistic philosophy)."[3] So the Word or Logos, who is Christ, preexistent with God before all else, is the "ultimate intelligibility of reality," that which provides order and structure and light and understanding to all creation, and through which all things were created. It's the God encountered by scientists and nature lovers, by hikers and astronomers, the God spoken to by poets, playwrights, and philosophers through the generations, who attest that the "world is charged with the grandeur of God."[4]

Many of us have an image of Jesus, and the gospel, that is decidedly smaller and more exclusive than the one that appears in John's Gospel, the Old Testament, and the early Christian creeds. This is not an accident. Much of the history of late modern Christianity, in both Catholic and Protestant circles, in reaction to cultural developments in society and the church trended toward a more exclusive understanding of who Christ is and how Christ is salvific. With Catholics, this exclusivity tends to manifest as belonging to the Catholic Church, or by being "in" or "out" of a state of grace. With Protestants, this might manifest as a specific creedal formula or understanding of justification and salvation, or, in evangelical circles, as a status of being "born again" in the spirit.

But God is bigger than any denomination's definition or delineation. And the best way to know this God is through prayer and belonging to a community of "pray-ers." One wise mentor once told me, "Faith isn't taught, faith is caught," meaning the best way to share your faith is to have a living and active faith in the first place. And I'm not talking about personality, I'm talking about lived spirituality. Many of us are not equipped to be extroverted, bubbly, hand-shaking and shoulder-slapping evangelists (least of all me). We certainly need them and the unique gifts that they bring, but we are not all called to be like them, and we are all called to evangelize. And even our silence can evangelize.

Getting to Know God's Goodness

A good starting point for this approach can be found in the long tradition of contemplative prayer in Catholicism. Many of our most effective and influential saints and doctors of the church were contemplatives, meaning they experienced God intimately during contemplative prayer, and this experience of God endured beyond what they could express in words. From Augustine to Aquinas, from Teresa of Avila to Teresa the Little Flower, from John the Evangelist to John of the Cross, from John Paul II to Oscar Romero, from Elizabeth of the Trinity to Dorothy Day, many of our greatest saints experienced a deep connection with God in prayer and were therefore the most influential in evangelizing and transforming the culture in which they lived.

And at the heart of the contemplative prayer tradition is the admonition "Be still and know that I am God." And how do we know that God is God? We know because we experience the divine presence within ourselves. In his *Confessions* St. Augustine wrote that God is "closer to me than I am to myself." St. Paul proclaimed that "It is no longer I who live, but Christ who lives in me." St. Gregory of Nyssa said that "God dwells in you, penetrates you, yet is not confined in you." St. John Paul II quoted the eleventh-century spiritual teacher Meister Eckhart: "Did not Eckhart teach his disciples: 'All God asks you most pressingly is to go out of yourself . . . and let God be God in you?" St. Catherine of Genoa said, "My only 'me' is God . . . in my soul I see nothing but God," and St. Teresa of Avila, doctor of the church and mystical teacher, wrote that in "total union, no separation is possible . . . when a little stream enters the sea, who could separate the waters back out again?" Her friend and confessor St. John of the Cross also wrote, "It seems to such a person . . . that the entire universe is an ocean of love in which one is engulfed; for conscious of the living center of love within, it is unable to catch sight of the boundaries of this love."[5]

God is within us, our deepest center is God, and all good prayer teaches us this. That same prayer might reveal to us our own shadow side, our own shortcomings, our own failures, and our own sins, but it will then lead us to the merciful embrace of the God who loves us and forgives us. We are all the prodigal son, we are all the woman caught in adultery. And as we experience the depth of God's goodness, love, and forgiveness in prayer, we discover, like Jacob, that: "Truly, the LORD is in this place and I did not know it . . . this is nothing else but the house of God, the gateway to heaven!" (Gen 28:17). We discover also through prayer, in ourselves and in others, that "the glory of God is the human person fully alive," to quote St. Irenaeus.

This is what I discovered most often as an RCIA director at a parish. As I met inquirers of all different backgrounds, together we would discover how God has been living and active in their life, often long before they ever approached the door of the parish office to inquire about the Catholic faith. And they would often discover that the God who brought them to Catholic faith is the same God that has always been with them. It was my same experience in prison ministry: we weren't "bringing God" to people, we were discovering God together in our loving relationship with one another. Both the minister and the one being ministered to were awakening to the presence of the God who has created them, formed them in God's image, and desires full and total union with them.

This is the power of the contemplative witness. It's a freedom from fear and coercion and an invitation to enter the silent love where God speaks to each of us. In the words of St. Augustine: "Let there be nothing between the soul and God." This is the calling of all who would evangelize: first, get to know God's goodness for yourself, and then you can share what you yourself have received.

I think we are in a contemplative renewal in the church, with eucharistic adoration, the rosary, centering prayer, Ignatian contemplation, and *lectio divina* becoming more and more popular among laypeople. We have so much noise in our everyday life, and so God seeks ever more to come to us in the silence, where we become silent, and God speaks to us in the still, silent peace of contemplative prayer.

This, of course, isn't the only place to discover God. I have learned much about God through direct service to people who are incarcerated in prison, or unhoused and sleeping on the streets, or struggling with addiction, or wounded by trauma. From these experiences, I've learned much about, as Pope Francis puts it, God's "style" and the "marks" of God's accompaniment: "closeness, compassion, and tenderness." It is to this reality of the gospel always being good news to the poor, and the ways we are evangelized through a witness of solidarity with the poor, that we will turn in the next chapter.

Questions for Reflection and Discussion

1. How does prayer influence your evangelization efforts? How is both shared liturgical prayer and silent prayer encouraged in your parish community?

2. Pope Francis states that God's "style" is "closeness, compassion, and tenderness." How do members of your parish community accompany one another with closeness, compassion, and tenderness? How could you grow?

Continuing the Conversation: The Fruits of Contemplative Prayer

Contemplative prayer offers a good counter to more panicked and fear-driven evangelization efforts. It helps us to see things with a wider lens, to acknowledge our own biases and become aware of blocks in our own perception of things.

Contemplative prayer is also imitative of the prayer life of Jesus, who regularly withdrew into the wilderness to pray. The Scriptures tell us that he would often pray all night long, and advised his disciples to not use too many words in prayer.

Another advantage of contemplative prayer is there are so many different kinds, and each one can appeal to the many different kinds of Catholics: meditation, eucharistic adoration, *lectio divina*, the rosary, centering prayer, or even simple silence before God, what Jesuit theologian Walter Burghardt described as a "long, loving look at the real."[6]

Consider the fruits of contemplative prayer in your life and in your own community. How is prayerful silence a part of your own spiritual life and your communal discernment together?

7

Good News for the Poor

*We have all known the long loneliness and we have
learned that the only solution is love and that love comes
with community.*

—Dorothy Day

Washing His Feet

He limped in off the street, leaning on a wheelchair that
had "2nd Floor Pain Clinic" written on the seat. On
the back, it just said "PAIN" in large letters.

We had just endured twelve days of subzero temperatures in Kansas City, with lows in the negative teens. At
Morning Glory Ministries, a social outreach ministry, we
had been struggling to help our guests amid the record
freeze and an ongoing pandemic.

I helped the man with the door, and he told me how many places he'd been kicked out of or shuffled around to. As he spoke, he sat down in the wheelchair. With a slow but steady determination he took off his old, battered shoe and the wet sock underneath, revealing a horrid sight: a missing big toe, the other toes blackened from frostbite, and crisscrossed scars running up the length of his leg.

PAIN, indeed.

After listening to his story, I spoke with our director and case worker, who would come up with a plan to help him find the care he needed. Around that time, a young woman came in for help. She said she'd lost everything and had been sleeping outside up until the previous evening, when it was just too cold to bear. In the middle of our conversation, the man in the wheelchair started crying. He was cold, in pain, and overwhelmed. I too was overwhelmed—by his acute suffering, by the suffering of all our guests, and by the cruelty of this particularly hard freeze.

I consoled him as best I could, and in between interviewing other guests, noticed the young woman had started talking to him, asking him why he was crying and what happened to his foot. When our case worker called him into his office, the woman pushed his wheelchair. And when they left the office with warm clothes, food, and housing resources in hand, she knelt in front of him, held his foot and carefully put on the dry sock and shoe he'd been given. She asked him if it felt okay. He nodded. Not only had he stopped crying, he almost smiled as she gently held his foot—and all his painful history—in her hands.

Moments like this make the resurrection believable. More than that, they make it possible, and maybe even inevitable—because on a freezing cold day in February, in the muddied vestibule of Morning Glory Ministries, I watched a young woman with nothing except her love, dignity, and compassion become Christ to someone who had even less. And in that moment, under the scourge of cold and in full view of the ravages of illness and injustice, I saw an indefatigable love pouring out of her and over all this world's brokenness.

She saw Christ, crucified in the flesh of our suffering brother, and she loved him. The promise of salvation that Easter offers is an invitation for us to do the same.[1]

The Word Became Flesh

I wrote the above reflection for the daily devotional *Give Us This Day*, and I include it here because I think it offers a helpful example of experiencing God and being evangelized by an encounter with the "other," by someone who might be marginalized or on the peripheries in society.

Many people who have participated in some form of outreach to people at the margins, be it in prison or hospital or homeless ministry, attest that one of the first things they learn is that they are not "bringing" God to the poor, sick, or imprisoned person. Indeed, one of the initial shocks of getting involved in these ministries, beyond the strangeness of the setting or situation, is the absolute abundance of God's grace, and even a felt experience of God's presence, through the person to whom we are ministering. "We get a lot more than we give," we often say. And we don't say this to romanticize, spiritualize, or sugarcoat the realities of illness, prison, or abject poverty. There are times when the suffering is overwhelming and disfiguring, and we are called to relieve it and alleviate it as best we can, all the while working to dismantle systems of sin and injustice in our world. But the spiritual reality remains: we often feel closer to God and nearer Christ when we draw near to those and walk with those on the margins of our society.

I think the reason for this is that Jesus was being incredibly literal when he said: "For I was hungry and you gave me food, I was thirsty and you gave me drink, a stranger and you welcomed me, naked and you clothed me, ill and you cared for me, in prison and you visited me" (Matt 25:31-45). Jesus Christ, the *Logos*, the preexistent reason for the intelligibility of all things, "through whom all things were made" and who holds all things together, became incarnate as a poor person among the poor, who formed the vast majority of his first disciples. He died as a poor person, utterly rejected. "Through him, with him, and in him, in the unity of the Holy Spirit," we are invited to encounter Christ in all things and in all places, but particularly in those people and places in which we might be tempted to believe that God is absent.

But if the Christ we are proclaiming is the same Christ that is found in John's Gospel, then that shouldn't surprise us, because the Christ who is the *Logos* or the Word of God knows each and every person and creature on the earth, and even in the entire universe. For "All things came to be through him, / and without him nothing came to be" (1:3). There isn't a single creature, soul, spirit, or human person who has not been created through Christ, who does not bear the mark of the creator, the imprint and intelligibility of the *Logos* on their body, soul, and spirit. Our more colonial evangelization efforts, both in the past and in today's world, forget this understanding and use religion as a tool for cultural conquest and social control.

Gaudium et Spes, the Vatican II Pastoral Constitution on the Church in the Modern World, expressed the reality that goodness, good will, and even the saving participation of all people in the paschal mystery outside the bounds of the church and even outside Christianity, when it said: "All this holds true not only for Christians but also for all people of good will in whose hearts grace is active invisibly. For since Christ died for everyone, and since all are in fact called to one and the same destiny, which is divine, we must hold that the holy Spirit offers to all the possibility of being made partners, in a way known to God, in the paschal mystery."[2] Pope Francis expands on this in *Gaudete et Exsultate*, his apostolic exhortation On the Call to Holiness in Today's World: "God is mysteriously present in the life of every person, in a way that he himself chooses, and we cannot exclude this by our presumed certainties. Even when someone's life appears completely wrecked, even when we see it devastated by vices or addictions, God is present there. If we let ourselves be guided by the Spirit rather than our own preconceptions, we can and must try to find the Lord in every human life."[3]

And Dwelt among Us

The witness of Jesus, a poor man with the poor, confirms this. In the Greco-Roman world at the time of Jesus, poverty was a sign of moral, social, and even spiritual inferiority. In that context, the idea that the poor could be "blessed" or "righteous" or even worth attending to at all with any moral, cultural, or religious seriousness was utterly alien to the elites of the Greco-Roman world, including the elites of Jesus's own Jewish culture (although it is deeply embedded in the Hebrew Scriptures, particularly the prophets). In that context, Jesus's inaugural message, his thesis statement for his ministry that he read at the synagogue in Nazareth, and the phrase from which we get the terms "good news" and "gospel" (and therefore "evangelization"), is focused on those experiencing material poverty:

> "The Spirit of the Lord is upon me,
> because he has anointed me
> to bring glad tidings to the poor.
> He has sent me to proclaim liberty to captives
> and recovery of sight to the blind,
> to let the oppressed go free,
> and to proclaim a year acceptable to the Lord." (Luke 4:18-19)

The "glad tidings" are the "good news," and in keeping with his inaugural message, Jesus was always bringing "glad tidings to the poor." Even the "year acceptable to the Lord" was focused on the poor, as it signaled a jubilee year in which all debts were forgiven. Debt was a powerful tool of social control and forced labor in the ancient world (as it is in our own). Those in debt who couldn't repay due to drought, famine, or misfortune would have been forced to sell themselves or their families into slavery. So the Jubilee Year would have been seen as a year of great rejoicing for the vast majority of poor, indebted peasants, and subversive to all those elites who held their debts. And indeed, after Jesus's inaugural address in which he quotes these verses from Isaiah, the people of Nazareth rise up against him, drive him out, and attempt "to hurl him down headlong" off of a cliff.

But Jesus also embraced rejection, and even suffering, torture, and death, as an essential part of his mission. Without it, the fullness of our understanding of who God is in Christ would not be revealed; as St. Paul reflects, the God revealed in Christ is a revelation of radical, self-emptying, sacrificial love:

> Christ Jesus,
> Who, though he was in the form of God,
> did not regard equality with God something to be grasped.
> Rather, he emptied himself,
> taking the form of a slave,
> coming in human likeness;
> and found human in appearance,
> he humbled himself,
> becoming obedient to death,
> even death on a cross. (Phil 2:5-8)

God reveals what True Love looks like on the cross: The radical message of the gospel, the reason for our evangelization efforts, is that the crucified Christ is one in being with the God of the transcendentals, the God preexisting before all creation, and indeed is the "ultimate intelligibility of all reality."[4] That same God assumed our humanity fully in the person of Christ, and lived among the poorest of the poor, and went to those who were most destitute, teaching that they were "blessed" and that God loves them, and indeed all of us, like a good and loving father.

This can't be understated: Jesus teaches us that God is *abba*: not a tyrant, not a despot, not a judge, but a loving parent, a loving and compassionate and caring mother and father. And like a good and loving parent, this God doesn't sit on the sidelines while people live in utter misery, thought to be forsaken and lost, by everyone, even God or the gods. Into this cultural understanding, Jesus comes to "seek and to save what is lost," and his ministry is filled with images of a shepherd seeking a lost sheep or a woman looking for a lost coin. Even in his death, the kind of death reserved for the very worst, the most forsaken, the most marginal in his society, Jesus the Christ saves us from ourselves, from death, from sin, and from all that would separate us from God. God offers Godself on the cross to reconcile us to Godself, and to "condemn the ruler of this world" who keeps us enchained.

This is the good news, and it's no wonder that it spread like wildfire among the slave quarters and catacombs of the ancient world. It's no wonder it's still spreading in prison cells, homeless shelters, rehab facilities, slums, and everywhere from which the comfortable of the world turn their gaze. The gospel, the good news, is indeed the glad tidings for the poor.

If our parishes are serious about evangelization, then they need to follow the example of Christ and become good news for the poor. It is to this end, becoming a credible witness to God's radical love in the world, our third principle for parish evangelization, that we will turn next.

Questions for Reflection and Discussion

1. Who in our parish community, and the wider community, are the poor, the vulnerable, and the marginalized? Who is kept on the periphery of our community?

2. How can our parishes become, or continue to be, good news to the poor? How can we reach out and be mutually evangelized by an encounter with the "other"? How has our accompaniment of the poor helped us encounter Christ?

3. Is our parish good news to the seeker, to the inquirer, to the person curious about faith in general? Why or why not?

Continuing the Conversation: Catholic Social Teaching

One of the ways the church has been good news to the poor is through the principles of Catholic social teaching. They have often been referred to as the "best kept secret" of Catholicism. Take a look at what the USCCB teaches about them here and examine how your parish is living these: https://www.usccb.org/beliefs-and-teachings /what-we-believe/catholic-social-teaching/seven-themes -of-catholic-social-teaching.

Part III

Evangelization Is a Radical and Credible Witness to God's Goodness

8

Becoming a Good News Parish

Love manifests itself in deeds more than words.

—*St. Ignatius of Loyola*

Neo-Gnostic Evangelization

One of the things Pope Francis points to as hampering evangelization efforts is what he calls "neo-Gnosticism." In *Gaudete et Exsultate*, his 2019 exhortation, he explains: "Gnostics think that their explanations can make the entirety of the faith and the Gospel perfectly comprehensible." I see this

87

often in would-be evangelizers: it's all about knowledge. It was a temptation I often fell into after my early conversion experiences. We can memorize the catechism or C. S. Lewis or G. K. Chesterton, or whatever book or author or YouTube video we prefer and start to believe that we can distill this millennia-old love affair between God and humanity into a few marketable soundbites. It's hubris.

Pope Francis counters this approach: "A healthy and humble use of reason in order to reflect on the theological and moral teaching of the Gospel is one thing. It is another to reduce Jesus' teaching to a cold and harsh logic that seeks to dominate everything. . . .When somebody has an answer for every question, it is a sign that they are not on the right road."[1] Again, in our current social media–driven conversations, we often seek to dominate, proving without a shadow of a doubt that our perspective on cultural issues, on Christianity, or on church politics is superior. But in doing so we pay a steep price, as our faith is reduced to yet another talking head that can easily be rejected or discarded. As Pope Francis reminds us, "throughout the history of the Church it has always been clear that a person's perfection is measured not by the information or knowledge they possess, but by the depth of their charity."[2]

It is this same measure, the depth of our charity, and the radical witness to that charity, that can also be applied to our parish's evangelization efforts. The degree to which our faith community is really living the gospel and, therefore, evangelizing, is the vital witness of our love for one another, for God, and for our neighbor. The inner nature of God in Godself, the nature of the Trinity, is love. And love presupposes a relationship of mutual exchange between distinct persons. Our God is not a monolith, not a set of rules and regulations that we must defend and protect. No, God is a community of love who invites us even more deeply into the divine nature, to share the love and joy of Father, Son, and Spirit in relationship with one another.

The image of God as Trinity has practical implications for how we live in community together and how we evangelize. Cardinal Blase Cupich, drawing on the work of theologian Meghan Clark, illustrates how a trinitarian understanding of God radiates outward from our parish communities: "These insights also have much to offer as we think about the church. Just as human beings are called to live in the image and likeness of the triune God, so too the church must mirror the life of the Trinity, never reducing our mission to projects and goals that are self-serving. The church too must reach out to the world and share the life that has been given to us."[3]

Reaching out to the world and sharing the life that has been given to us calls for a radical witness. Most of us are a bit suspect of the word "radical," as it's been widely denigrated in the media and normally denotes someone who is an ideologue. But the word "radical" just means "going to the roots," "going to the origin," or having to do with that which is the most vital and essential. In the case of Christian evangelization, the origin, the roots, and that which is most vital is Christ, who reveals to us the unstoppable goodness, mercy, truth, and beauty of God most radically on the cross in a total act of self-giving love in the face of cruelty, brutality, and evil.

Our parishes, our church, and each of us are similarly called to be radical witnesses, a visible sign of the "kingdom bubbling forth," to imitate the self-giving, self-emptying love of Christ on the cross in the face of world's indifference, and to be visible and trustworthy signs of God's love in our witness. How is your parish called to be an evangelizing witness? In the next section, we'll explore how to share God's goodness in your parish community and challenge yourself to discern how the Holy Spirit is calling your community to grow in your witness.

A Tale of Two Parishes

One day during daily Mass at the Cathedral of the Immaculate Conception in downtown Kansas City, Missouri, a young man walked in off the street wearing only some long underwear and a tank top. He was totally barefoot, and it was freezing outside, with temperatures in the low twenties and a bitter cold rain falling. The man was obviously struggling and looking for assistance. I approached him and asked if he had come here for warm clothes and food, and he said yes. "I was told to go to the Gold Dome."

I walked him over to Morning Glory Ministries, our outreach to the homeless and working poor. I led him to our emergency assistance area, gave him some warm clothes, thick wool socks, shoes, a jacket with hat and gloves, and some food. He ate it in the warmth of the office, and I told him about the help we could provide with identification, with housing, and with job placement if he was interested. He nodded while he ate, and then promptly left, belly full and fully clothed for the cold day. I never saw him again.

When I told the director of Morning Glory that I'd found the man during Mass and brought him over, he said, "You encountered Jesus at Mass and then you encountered him again when you brought him here to be fed and clothed."

That was the daily reality of our ministry at the Cathedral of the Immaculate Conception. Fr. Paul Turner, the pastor, would often say that the parish had two lungs: our liturgy and our outreach to the poorest of the poor in our community. Each day I breathed deeply with both lungs, and during my time there, I experienced a deep sense that this is what the gospel is supposed to look like, that *this* is how it is supposed to be lived: encountering Christ in the liturgy and the community gathered for worship, and encountering Christ in the poor who came to us for food, for warmth, for clothing and housing, as well as for a kind word, a hug, an acknowledgement of their inherent human dignity. It was, and still is, an integrated and authentic Christian witness.

The parish I work at now, Church of the Nativity, is at the other end of the spectrum. It's located in a wealthy suburb in Leawood, Kansas, across the state line and in another diocese from the Cathedral. It's an entirely different culture, with different gifts and resources and different challenges to consider. While occasionally we might have someone who walks into the church to ask for help, it's very rare, and we normally point them toward Catholic Charities or help in a different way.

At Nativity, most of the parish budget goes to support the growing school, which provides the essential ministry of a Catholic education for the children in the community. At the same time, we are a resource-rich parish, with incredibly accomplished, talented, and committed parishioners who have started a variety of ministries to serve the community. In Kansas, there is a foster care crisis, and in response, parishioners have begun mobilizing to support foster families, provide respite care for foster families, and serve as emergency foster parents to children who are just entering the system. But the problem is Goliath-sized, and touches on issues of generational poverty, the criminal justice system, access to health care and housing, and so much more. We are currently going through a discernment process to decide how we are uniquely called to respond to thousands of children who fall through the cracks of the system every year.

Every parish is unique, and every parish is different. That's why no one-size-fits-all approach will work when it comes to evangelization. But every parish is called to be credible witnesses of God's goodness in our community, especially to those who are suffering in any way. And so every parish, parish staff, and parish community is called to read the signs of the times, the events shaping our world, our city, and our neighborhood, and discern what the Holy Spirit is calling us to do in response.

Three Key Questions

Each parish, like each one of us, is uniquely called to respond to God's invitation. And this response often starts in small ways. Morning Glory Ministries began with a parish secretary at the Cathedral who encountered hungry people every day outside of the parish office. She began making peanut butter sandwiches at home and bringing them to work, distributing them throughout the day to her guests. Fast forward a decade, and it was a thriving ministry feeding hundreds each day and serving thousands each year. It has saved and transformed lives and it continues to do so.

What is the unique vocation of your parish? What's your peanut butter sandwich? All of us are certainly called to engage in the rich sacramental and liturgical life of the church together, to proclaim God's word, and to accompany and care for our parishioners. That's a given. But perhaps your parish also has a food kitchen or a parish school or another outreach ministry where you engage the community. Maybe you have a vibrant social event and faith formation calendar, with abundant opportunities for growing in discipleship and fellowship together. Wherever and whatever state your parish is in, it is always fruitful to discuss the question, "What is God calling us to do at this time?"

And that's a question of discernment, of prayerfully paying attention to our own desires, emotions, and listening for the "still, small voice" within. When discussing discernment and vocation, I've often found it helpful to refer to a talk on vocation given by the late Fr. Michael Himes, an award-winning professor of theology at Boston College. While Fr. Himes was discussing our individual vocation, we can adapt his insights for communal discernment as well. In a lecture, Fr. Himes came up with "Three Key Questions" to ask when we are trying to discern our vocation. They are, first, what gives you joy? Second, are you good at it? And third, does anybody need you to do it?[4]

Often, we go about the question of vocation backwards. We think, what will people pay me to do or what will make me a lot of money? Then, we try to figure out what we can do well enough to make said money. Whether or not it's a source of joy or "deep gladness" is relegated to either the very last question we ask or to total irrelevancy.

We often do the same thing in parish life, especially as it concerns evangelization. We think, what do we need to do to get people back to church, or, will people come back after the pandemic? We rarely ask ourselves, is there any joy here for people to come back to? And if so, what is it? What is our overflowing joy, our deep gladness, as a parish?

Our vocation, in the words of Frederick Buechner, is where "deep gladness and the world's deep hunger meet," and so we should pay attention to the movements of the Holy Spirit and the signs of the Holy Spirit's presence when we consider to what and to whom God is calling us. So I would propose a process in which the parish community is invited to discern their unique vocation using questions about our parish's joy, gifts, and the needs of the community:

1. Joy: What gives this parish community joy? What ministries, liturgies, services, and outreach helps us experience God's love? What events, liturgies, shared prayer experiences, and outreach increases our hope and faith as a community? What excites us about belonging to this parish?

2. Gifts: What are the charisms, or gifts, of our parish community? What do we do really well? What do we

do that no other parish could do? What do visitors and guests to our parish say about us?

3. Community: What are the needs of the community, both within our parish and outside our parish? Who are the people in most need, or who are suffering the most spiritually, financially, relationally, or emotionally? Where are the places of suffering, of hurt, of conflict and division to which we can bring the light of Christ? How are we being called to give of ourselves and share our gifts? What's your "peanut butter sandwich," your small step to serving the world?

When you've asked these questions of your parish, with your pastors, staff, and parishioners, you'll have a good idea of what your unique parish vocation might be. Of course, you should do this all in the context of prayer, of listening to the Holy Spirit, and reading the signs of the times in community.

In my experience, this isn't done often enough. We rarely sit down and prayerfully discern together where the Holy Spirit is leading us. We often either simply want to "maintain" what is going on at the church, or we want to do something radically different and go out on "mission."

In the next chapter, we'll discuss this and provide a few models of an evangelizing church, illustrating how our operative image, or model, of church affects how we evangelize and encounter the culture in which we find ourselves.

Questions for Reflection and Discussion

1. It's always helpful to reflect on your own vocation as you look to discern how your community is being called. Answer the three key questions for yourself:
   a. What gives you joy?
   b. What are you good at?
   c. Does anybody need you to do it?

2. How does our parish walk with parishioners who are struggling? Is our parish welcoming, hospitable, and inclusive? How are people nourished, physically and spiritually, here?

Continuing the Conversation: Your Parish's Vocation

Take a look at the three key questions. Which resonates most with your parish?

a. Joy: What gives this parish community joy? What ministries, liturgies, services, and outreach help us experience God's love? What events, liturgies, shared prayer experiences, and outreach increase our hope and faith as a community? What excites us about belonging to this parish?

b. Gifts: What are the charisms, or gifts, of our parish community? What do we do really well? What do we do that no other parish could do? What do visitors and guests to our parish say about us?

c. Community: What are the needs of the community, both within our parish and outside our parish? Who are the people in most need, or who are suffering the most spiritually, financially, relationally, or emotionally? Where are the places of suffering, of hurt, of conflict and division to which we can bring the light of Christ?

9

Models of a Good News Church

*It is precisely this path of synodality which God expects
of the Church of the third millennium.*

—*Pope Francis*[1]

Fortress Faith

While reading a recent capital campaign pamphlet for a
new church in my area, I noticed that it promised, among
other things, to build a new and "unapologetically Catholic"
church that would serve as a "fortress of faith" for this as
well as future generations. And while I found the design
for the church both beautiful and appealing (although a
baldacchino in Missouri feels a little, well, forced), I found

the language around this campaign a bit off-putting. I did a little more digging and found that many of the donors and those connected with the campaign had a particular view, or model, of the church in mind as they sought to build a new one: a fortress.

I got to thinking: what is a fortress for, and how would a "fortress church" fulfill the mission of the gospel? Fortresses have huge walls and imposing defenses: they are bulwarks against something that would seek to destroy them. They protect something or someone who is too valuable to be left outside to the enemy or the elements.

But how could a fortress fulfill the mission of Jesus, which calls us to be witnesses to God's radical, incarnational, self-emptying love in the world? A fortress would be a welcome sight to those fleeing persecution or oppression if they were fearful for their lives or their family members. A fortress would be helpful if a person needed protection, safety, security, and stability, or if they were running from an enemy. But a fortress church would be a sanctuary only if you were already inside, or if you knew you had access. For all those left outside the walls, whether they be helpless or malicious, the fortress would be an imposing sign of their own exclusion, their own lack of belonging. Fortresses might protect, but they also exclude: they protect by separating and dividing.

A different image of the church is found in the writings of Pope Francis: the field hospital. "The thing the church needs most today is the ability to heal wounds and to warm the hearts of the faithful; it needs nearness, proximity. I see the church as a field hospital after battle. . . . Heal the wounds, heal the wounds. . . . And you have to start from the ground up."[2]

A field hospital is radically different from a fortress. It doesn't have imposing defenses, probably just some canvas sheets and tent poles, and it's incredibly mobile. A field hospital would be appealing if you were on the outside looking in, especially if you were wounded. It would mean life and healing. While it would provide some protection from the elements, its primary purpose would be healing, not defense. And it wouldn't seek to protect what it had so much as to give what it could, especially to those who were most wounded.

There are some limitations even to this image, however, no matter how appealing we might find it. For one, I would imagine that we ministers, lay and ordained, would be considered the medics and doctors in the field hospital. So we "healers" would have all the expertise and equipment necessary to attend to the "wounded." But, in my experience, we "healers" are often just as wounded as those who come to us. But that's okay, because if we follow the example of the Risen Christ, who bears the marks of crucifixion that have been utterly transfigured by God's love, we know that we can be wounded healers in the world.

Models of Church

But there are even more models and images of church that can connect with an evangelizing parish. Theologian Cardinal Avery Dulles, SJ, created a groundbreaking ecclesial framework for understanding different visions of the church in *Models of the Church* (1974). For the post–Vatican II church, it offered a helpful and complementary framework in which any Catholic, lay or ordained, conservative or liberal, could find themselves. The models were drawn from his own research into ecclesiology as well as from the documents of the Second Vatican Council, particularly *Lumen Gentium*, which outlined the rich history and self-understanding of the church in a return to the sources of that self-understanding in history. The models are both complementary and illuminating, and you might find different elements of each in your own parish community. We will briefly examine each in light of the call to be an evangelizing parish community.

The first model of the church is the Church as Mystical Communion: "The goal of the Church . . . is a spiritual or supernatural one. The Church aims to lead men [and women] into communion with the divine."[3] This model also combines two other images, the church as the people of God and the church as the Body of Christ. We are united as one people of God by our divine, eucharistic communion in Christ. This model might also emphasize openness, a certain dynamism of relationships, and a combination of both the vertical (God-human) and horizontal (human-human) aspects of our community life together. It's a helpful model for evangelization, as it loses sight of neither the human nor the divine aspects of our communal life together, and beautifully connects our model of church with our liturgy, the source and summit of our faith.

The second model of church is the Church as a Sacrament, and this helpfully uses the church's own language to understand better the call of the church in the world. A sacrament is "an outward sign instituted by Christ to give grace." The church, then, as a sacrament, is called to be a visible sign of the graced community that Christ established through his life, death, and resurrection. We are called to be a visible sign (or a witness) of Christ present in the world today, and of God's desire for community with all peoples and, indeed, with all of creation. This model beautifully incorporates the visible (human, communal) and invisible (divine, supernatural) together as well, without too clearly separating them. Like Christ, we hold the mystery of divinity and humanity together in the mystery of the church as sacrament. Isn't this a reality we experience at every Mass?

The third model of church is the Church as Institution. This is perhaps the most visible and immediately understandable model of church. It equates the various institutional elements of the church, such as canon law, liturgical norms, offices, and hierarchies as the very nature of the church. Cardinal Dulles warned against this being the most operative or primary model of church. If it is, the church becomes "rigid, doctrinaire, and conformist; it could easily substitute the official Church for God, and this would be a form of idolatry."[4] Any model that looks at only the visible elements of the church or emphasizes the distinction between the various "classes" in the church might also be closely connected with an institutional model. The "fortress" image of the faith might also overly emphasize the institutional church. But, while an overt focus on the institutional church is a temptation to idolatry and spiritual narcissism, we throw out these institutional elements at our own risk, as they are essential to our stability, our community, and without them, it would be hard to find a common rulebook for our communal life together.

The fourth model of church is the Church as Herald, which ties in closely with our focus on evangelization. A herald is a messenger of a king, so in this case, it is the church as a herald of Christ the King, fulfilling the great commission to "Go out and make disciples of all nations." This model owes a huge debt to our Protestant sisters and brothers, who have made a focus on the Word of God in Scripture and proclaiming it to the wider world a primary goal. Cardinal Dulles warned that this model had shortcomings if it wasn't backed up with service that would help build a better world, if it "focuses too exclusively on witness to the neglect of action. It is too pessimistic or quietistic with regard to the possibilities of human effort to establish a better human society in this life, and the duty of Christians to take part in this common effort."[5]

The fifth model addresses this concern for social justice, when it looks at the Church as Servant. In this understanding, the church is called to follow in the footsteps of Jesus Christ: "[T]he Church announces the coming of the Kingdom not only in word, through preaching and proclamation, but more particularly in work, in her ministry of reconciliation, of binding up wounds, of suffering service, of healing. . . . And the Lord was the 'man for others,' so must the Church be 'the community for others.'"[6] We might also consider this model to have a deep resonance with the "field hospital" image as well, with its focus on healing and binding up those who are broken.

Later in life Cardinal Dulles offered a sixth model, the Church as the Community of Disciples. This model places Jesus and a personal relationship with him at the center of our church community, in which we always strive to grow closer to Christ in all that we do. There is a particular resonance here with evangelization initiatives, even series like the Chosen, as well as the Spiritual Exercises of St. Ignatius, all of which try to facilitate a personal and intimate encounter with Christ, like those experienced by the first disciples and apostles. It also calls us to *discipleship* and imitation of Christ, including sharing in his suffering for the salvation of the world.

The Best Model Is All of Them

Which is the best model of church as it relates to evangelization? Quite simply, all of them, together, because in each of these models of church, there is present another possible touchpoint of evangelization as we encounter one another and the world. As we gather together at Sunday Mass, is a mystical communion of the visible and invisible present? And does this ripple outward in our attitudes toward each other the other days of the week? Similarly, are our parish, our diocese, and our universal church sacraments and visible signs of God's love for humanity? If so, how is this love made manifest, made incarnate, in our good works? Does our church community serve the greater community, especially those at the peripheries? Do we announce the gospel, the good news, to all we meet? Or are we too timid to proclaim Christ crucified as the reason for our gathering, our service, our love for one another?

An overemphasis on any particular model is a possible danger, a temptation to idolatry, irrelevancy, or total dissolution and division. Therefore, any truly Catholic approach to evangelization would involve a healthy, lifegiving, and fruitful integration of all these models, because while we are announcing the gospel of Jesus Christ, we are aware that in many ways, for the people we encounter, the medium is the message. Our communities, the way we treat and love one another, who is included and who is excluded, the way we witness to God's goodness in the world, the way we work in society to make it more humane and just, the way we worship and encounter God in the gift of the sacraments, and the visible and invisible signs of our communion with God in Christ and with each other, with all the saints living and dead: all of these are ways in which our communities both announce the good news and become it, because the good news is God, and God is drawing all creation to fulfillment in complete union with God in Christ. This is our mission as a church, our mission given by Christ to become the good news of salvation: "[B]y the power of the risen Lord [the church] is given strength to overcome, in patience and in love, its sorrows and its difficulties, both those that are from within and those that are from without, so that it may reveal in the world, faithfully, although with shadows, the mystery of its Lord until, in the end, it shall be manifested in full light."[7]

An Old and New Image: A Synodal Church

But there's another new image of the church that is emerging. In the later part of 2021 Pope Francis officially launched the Synod on Synodality, the largest consultative process in human history and possibly the most consequential ecclesial process since the Second Vatican Council. And almost nobody knew anything about it.

After reading the Preparatory Documents for the synod, I wrote *Your Church Wants to Hear from You: What Is the Synod on Synodality?* in an attempt to get the word out about the synod to as many Catholics as quickly as possible. I was energized by the idea of being a "Listening Church," because most of my experience as both a layperson and minister was a church that the church only preached; it rarely listened. And also because in childhood, one of the formative experiences I had of the church were the quiet whispers we used to hear as kids about *this* parish or *this* family or *this* priest. Eventually, the whispers became not so quiet as the sexual abuse crisis broke, and suddenly the preaching we'd always heard rang especially hollow, and the decision to disaffiliate, consciously or unconsciously, seemed especially enticing.

In spite of all this, I love the church. The liturgy remains the taproot of my joy, and the sacramental experience of being Catholic remains the bedrock for my understanding of who God is and who I am in God. I love the opportunity to collaborate with diverse people from all over the world, and the church continues to encourage me to find God in all things in prayer, to be a consistent and radical witness to God's love, especially for the poor and marginal, and to learn and probe its rich intellectual history. But often, when it comes to intra-church issues, I feel like we fall short of what we could be. We rarely talk about the good we do. We rarely talk at all, to be honest, at least to one another about real and serious concerns we may have about the church and how we are church with one another.

Often those who are most outspoken among us represent the most narrow-minded and shallow version of what it means to be Catholic and Christian. Our hierarchy, at least in the U.S., often seems to cater to politically motivated ideologues, or those who, rather conveniently, fill the diocesan coffers during annual appeals. Left behind are the vast majority of Catholics, both practicing and disaffiliated. People of all ages are running out the door and we never bother to ask them: Why, after a lifetime of Catholic education, of Catholic practice, of Catholic devotion, are you leaving now?

It's rarely ever about Jesus, or God, or the gospel, or even the Eucharist. Former Catholics continue to love Jesus, and God, and communion. And most of us know this, though we fear to admit it. Many of us in ministry have lost a lot of our joy, our trust in one another, and a lot of our public credibility. It is not an easy time to be Catholic, or to be working in Catholic ministry. And that's exactly why we are being called to be more synodal, and indeed, to become a synodal church: "It is precisely this path of *synodality* which God expects of the Church of the third millennium. . . . A synodal Church is a Church which listens, which realizes that listening 'is more than simply hearing.' It is a mutual listening in which everyone has something to learn."[8]

We all prefer the comfort of our own echo chambers, and so it's going to take a lot of practice for all of us to learn how to be more synodal. And while we are called to correction and accountability and truth-telling, there is often at least a hint of the hard truth we need to hear in the encounter with the other person: "What the Lord is asking of us is already in some sense present in the very word 'synod.' Journeying together—laity, pastors, the Bishop of Rome—is an easy concept to put into words, but not so easy to put into practice."[9]

A synodal church is the only church capable of reading the signs of the times accurately, and more importantly, listening to the call of the Holy Spirit in response to those signs. Without synodality, we become ossified, reactionary, and totally unable to engage and evangelize the culture. The path isn't easy, but a synodal church is an evangelizing church, because only a synodal church draws on the unique charisms of the entire community. And we will need everyone if we hope to become the good news we proclaim.

Questions for Reflection and Discussion

1. Which model of church do you find most attractive? Which do you find least attractive? Which models do you see most clearly and prominently in your parish community and in your diocese?

2. Is your parish a synodal church? Do people feel welcome, listened to, and included? Does your parish and diocese walk together?

3. Who is excluded from our church communities? Whom do we refuse to walk with? How is Jesus calling us to encounter those on the "peripheries" of our parish communities?

Continuing the Conversation: Synodal Questions

Take a look at the questions adapted from the Synod on Synodality below. Think about your own parish community and answer the questions truthfully.

1. Companions on the Journey: A synodal church "journeys together" and makes sure no one is left behind, being welcoming and accompanying. Is this your experience of church?

2. A Listening Church: A synodal church is a listening church. A synodal church listens to all, with an open mind and heart. It creates space for laity, especially women, young people, and those on the margins of society. Is this your experience of church? Why or why not?

3. Communication: A synodal church promotes free and authentic communication within the community, inviting

everyone to speak with courage, truth, and charity. Is this your experience of church?

4. Celebrating: A synodal church "journeys together" because of our shared experience of liturgy, prayer, and the Eucharist. All are encouraged to participate fully and actively in the liturgical life of the church, and liturgy inspires us to discern and discuss together. Is this your experience of church?

5. Shared Sense of Mission: A synodal church shares a sense of mission among all the baptized, and the community supports the work of those who pursue social justice, who pursue scientific research, who teach, who promote human rights, and who protect the environment. Is this your experience of church?

6. Dialogue in the Community: A synodal church dialogues both within the community and with the larger society, addressing differences of opinion, vision, and experience with charity, and promoting dialogue with the poor and marginalized. Is this your experience of church?

7. Dialogue with other Christians: A synodal church feels united in one baptism with other Christians, producing good fruit by journeying together. Is this your experience of church?

8. Authority and Participation: A synodal church fosters participation and a shared sense of mission, with authority exercised in a synodal style at the parish and diocesan level, and the voices of the laity upheld. Is this your experience of church?

9. Discerning and Deciding: A synodal church makes decisions in a synodal way, that is, through discernment, listening to one another and the Spirit, and gathering consensus within our hierarchically structured communities, promoting greater transparency and accountability. Is this your experience of church?

10. Forming Ourselves in Synodality: A synodal church forms people to listen and engage in dialogue. Is this your experience of church?

Conclusion: Parishes Are Real Places

One of my favorite TV shows is the long-running British comedy *Doc Martin*. It's about a misanthropic, highly intellectual surgeon from London who becomes the general practitioner of a small Cornish village on the coast. In the first few episodes, he discovers that the quaint appearance of the village hides a web of drama and human relationships built on survival, convenience, bitter grudges, and deception. As Doc Martin attempts to navigate these, he experiences fierce blowback for his many faux pas and makes error after error in relating to people there.

When he informs his aunt that he is leaving the village because of all this, she responds starkly: "If you wanted a chocolate box village, go to the Isle of Wight. This is a real place."

I've often thought about that phrase while writing this book. Parishes are real places. And while there is a temptation in our evangelization efforts to make our parishes into something fake, something a bit like the "chocolate box village" or a touristy liturgical theme park, the reality of our parish life, of the complications and conflict that always comes with life in community, will always catch up with us.

The three principles of parish evangelization outlined in this book are not attempts to make our parishes fake or artificial. They are ways that I hope will make our parishes *more real*.

When I say that "everything is a touchpoint of evangelization," it doesn't mean that every encounter has to be perfect. It means that there is room for humility, authenticity, and even apology, in each and every encounter. We don't have to be doormats, but we are called to be doorways that open up to the infinite love of God that we hope to share with others. We might have to say "Jesus, take the (evangelizing) wheel" during highly charged encounters in ministry, and that's okay. God can use our weakness.

When I say that "evangelization is discovering the radical goodness of God," it isn't to deny that all of us will have to walk through those dark valleys of suffering, tragedy, or experiences of God's absence. We are sometimes called to walk those difficult paths, and in doing so we become good companions to others who might be experiencing the same. We are, after all, called to be wounded healers, like Christ, and Christ can use our wounds to share the gospel with others.

And finally, when I say that "evangelization is a radical and credible witness to God's love," it doesn't mean that our parishes, and we ourselves, won't often fall short of that witness. We are human, we are weak, we are divided and sinful. That's a given. But God loves us in our human weakness. And failure teaches us to be humble, to rely more and more on one another, on the community of faith, and on God. Failure also teaches us that we can be vulnerable, and that we can be loved unconditionally, especially when we feel unlovable.

One of my favorite books from childhood is *The Velveteen Rabbit*, about a boy's beloved stuffed animal that becomes a "real" rabbit because the boy loves him so much (full disclosure: I had a stuffed animal raccoon named Ricky that looked an awful lot like this rabbit after years of snuggling). In the book, the little stuffed rabbit is told by the wise old rocking horse that "love makes us real." I think that's true of each of us, and true of our parish communities, and indeed, of the entire church as well: Love makes us real.

And that's the hope of this book: that the love of Christ, poured out for each of us, helps us, and our parishes, become more real. And real parishes filled with real people are our greatest hope for becoming and sharing the good news with the world.

September 29, 2022

Feast of Saints Michael, Gabriel, and Raphael

Notes

Introduction

1. Monique Beals, "The Fastest Growing US Religious Affiliation? 'None,' Poll Says," *The Hill*, December 14, 2021, https://thehill.com/homenews/state-watch/585764-the-fastest-growing-us-religious-affiliation-none-poll-says/.

2. Synod of Bishops, *For a Synodal Church: Communion, Participation, and Mission*, Preparatory Document for the Synod 2021–2023, https://www.synod.va/en/news/the-preparatory-document.html.

3. Pope Francis, "Address at the Opening of the Synod of Bishops on Young People, the Faith, and Vocational Discernment," October 3, 2018, http://secretariat.synod.va/content/synod2018/en/news/address-by-pope-francis-at-the-opening-of-the-synod-of-bishops-.html.

Chapter 1

1. Pope Francis, *Evangelii Gaudium* (November 24, 2013), 94, https://www.vatican.va/content/francesco/en/apost_exhortations/documents/papa-francesco_esortazione-ap_20131124_evangelii-gaudium.html.

2. *Evangelii Gaudium*, 95.

Chapter 2

1. Paraphrasing Jürgen Moltmann, *The Church in the Power of the Spirit: A Contribution to Messianic Ecclesiology* (London: SCM Press, 1977), 64.

2. Moltmann, *Church in the Power*, 64.

3. Soli Salgado, "At Inaugural Conference, Spanish-Speaking Scholars Focus on Globalization, Exclusion," *National Catholic Reporter*, February 24, 2017, https://www.ncronline.org/news/theology/inaugural -conference-spanish-speaking-scholars-focus-globalization-exclusion.

4. David Bentley Hart, "Christ's Rabble," *Commonweal*, September 27, 2016, https://www.commonwealmagazine.org/christs-rabble.

5. Antonio Spadaro, SJ, "What Is the Church's Vocation? Pope Francis in Conversation with the Maltese Jesuits," *La Civiltà Cattolica*, April 15, 2022, https://www.laciviltacattolica.com/what-is-the-churchs -vocation-pope-francis-in-conversation-with-the-maltese-jesuits/.

6. Pope Paul VI, *Evangelii Nuntiandi* (December 8, 1975), 14, https:// www.vatican.va/content/paul-vi/en/apost_exhortations/documents/hf _p-vi_exh_19751208_evangelii-nuntiandi.html.

7. Joseph Cardinal Ratzinger, "The New Evangelization, Building the Civilization of Love," December 12, 2000, https://www.piercedhearts .org/benedict_xvi/Cardinal%20Ratzinger/new_evangelization.htm.

8. *Lumen Gentium* (November 21, 1964), 3, in Austin Flannery, ed., *Vatican Council II: Constitutions, Decrees, Declarations; The Basic Sixteen Documents* (Collegeville, MN: Liturgical Press, 2014).

9. *Lumen Gentium*, 8.

10. *Lumen Gentium*, 5.

11. Contemporary translation of St. Athanasius, On the Incarnation, 54: "For He was made man that we might be made God."

12. Antonio Spadaro, SJ, "What Is the Church's Vocation? Pope Francis in Conversation with the Maltese Jesuits," La Civiltà Cattolica, April 15, 2022, https://www.laciviltacattolica.com/what-is-the-churchs -vocation-pope-francis-in-conversation-with-the-maltese-jesuits/.

13. *Lumen Gentium*, 34.

14. *Lumen Gentium*, 3.

15. *Catechism of the Catholic Church*, 2nd ed. (United States Catholic Conference—Libreria Editrice Vaticana, 1997), 853.

16. *Catechism of the Catholic Church*, 853.

17. Spadaro, "What Is the Church's Vocation?"

18. Massimiliano Menichetti, "Pope Francis in Canada: The Gift of Tears," *Vatican News*, August 3, 2022, https://www.vaticannews.va/en/pope/news/2022-08/pope-francis-canada-gift-tears-indigenous-people-penitential.html.

Chapter 3

1. Pope Francis, apostolic letter *Desiderio Desideravi* (June 29, 2022), 4, https://www.vatican.va/content/francesco/en/apost_letters/documents/20220629-lettera-ap-desiderio-desideravi.html.

2. *Desiderio Desideravi*, 11.

3. Leo the Great, *Sermo LXIII*: De Passione Domini III, 7. Quoted in *Desiderio Desideravi*, 41.

4. *General Instruction of the Roman Missal* (Washington, DC: United States Conference of Catholic Bishops, 2003), 16 (hereafter referred to as GIRM).

5. GIRM, 5.

6. GIRM, 78.

7. *Lumen Gentium* (November 21, 1964), 40, in Austin Flannery, ed., *Vatican Council II: Constitutions, Decrees, Declarations; The Basic Sixteen Documents* (Collegeville, MN: Liturgical Press, 2014).

8. Paul Turner, *My Sacrifice and Yours: Our Participation in the Eucharist* (Chicago: Liturgy Training Publications, 2016), 16.

9. Turner, *My Sacrifice and Yours*, 23.

10. *Lumen Gentium*, 34, emphasis added.

11. Pope Francis, "Address to Teachers and Students of the Pontifical Liturgical Institute" (May 7, 2022), https://www.vatican.va/content/francesco/en/speeches/2022/may/documents/20220507-pont-istituto-liturgico.html.

12. Francis, "Address Pontifical Liturgical Institute."

13. Francis, "Address Pontifical Liturgical Institute."

14. Francis, "Address Pontifical Liturgical Institute."

15. Francis, "Address Pontifical Liturgical Institute."

16. Michael J. Sanem, Incarnation Is Everywhere, www.incarnation iseverywhere.com.

17. *Desiderio Desideravi*, 42.

18. Francis, "Address Pontifical Liturgical Institute."

19. Leo, *Sermo LXIII*, 7, quoted in *Desiderio Desideravi*, 41.

Chapter 4

1. Pope Francis, *Evangelii Gaudium* (November 24, 2013), 288, https://www.vatican.va/content/francesco/en/apost_exhortations/documents/papa-francesco_esortazione-ap_20131124_evangelii-gaudium.html.

2. Fr. Peter Marsalek, DISCIPLE: Formed in Holiness, Becoming Missionary Disciples, https://becomingmissionarydisciples.net/about-disciple. Used by permission.

3. Marsalek, DISCIPLE.

4. Marsalek.

5. Marsalek.

6. For more on synodality, see Michael J. Sanem, *Your Church Wants to Hear from You: What Is the Synod on Synodality?* (Collegeville, MN: Liturgical Press, 2022); and www.synod.va.

Chapter 5

1. "Youth Ranking 2022," Mental Health America, https://www.mhanational.org/issues/2022/mental-health-america-youth-data.

2. *Catechism of the Catholic Church*, 2nd ed. (United States Catholic Conference—Libreria Editrice Vaticana, 1997), 214.

3. *Catechism of the Catholic Church*, 41, quoting Wis 13:5.

4. *Catechism of the Catholic Church*, 42, quoting the Anaphora of the *Liturgy of St. John Chrysostom*.

Chapter 6

1. Gregory of Nazianzus, Epistle 101.

2. Gregory of Nazianzus, *Orationes* 1, 5.

3. New American Bible, Revised Edition, footnote to John 1:1, accessed at https://bible.usccb.org/bible/john/1.

4. Gerard Manley Hopkins, "God's Grandeur," https://www.poetry foundation.org/poems/44395/gods-grandeur.

5. This entire paragraph is a paraphrase of chapter 2 of Martin Laird's wonderful *An Ocean of Light: Contemplation, Transformation, and Liberation* (New York: Oxford University Press, 2018), essential reading for anyone interested in the contemplative tradition and entering into contemplative prayer. He is a very able, wise, and compassionate guide.

6. Walter Burghardt, "Contemplation: A Long Loving Look at the Real," in George W. Traub, *An Ignatian Spirituality Reader* (Chicago: Loyola Press, 2008; originally published in 1989), 89–98.

Chapter 7

1. Michael J. Sanem, "Washing His Feet," *Give Us This Day*, April 2022, http://www.giveusthisday.org (Collegeville, MN: Liturgical Press, 2022). Used with permission.

2. *Gaudium et Spes* (December 7, 1965), 22, in Austin Flannery, ed., *Vatican Council II: Constitutions, Decrees, Declarations; The Basic Sixteen Documents* (Collegeville, MN: Liturgical Press, 2014).

3. Pope Francis, *Gaudete et Exsultate* (March 19, 2018), 42, https:// www.vatican.va/content/francesco/en/apost_exhortations/documents /papa-francesco_esortazione-ap_20180319_gaudete-et-exsultate.html.

4. New American Bible, Revised Edition, footnote to John 1:1, accessed at https://bible.usccb.org/bible/john/1.

Chapter 8

1. Pope Francis, *Gaudete et Exsultate* (March 19, 2018), 39, 41, https:// www.vatican.va/content/francesco/en/apost_exhortations/documents /papa-francesco_esortazione-ap_20180319_gaudete-et-exsultate.html.

2. Francis, *Gaudete et Exsultate*, 37.

3. Cardinal Blasé J. Cupich, "Preaching on the Trinity," *Chicago Catholic*, June 15, 2022, https://www.chicagocatholic.com/cardinal

-blase-j.-cupich/-/article/2022/06/15/preaching-on-the-trinity. He refers to Meghan Clark's book *The Vision of Catholic Social Thought: The Virtue of Solidarity and the Praxis of Human Rights*.

4. Fr. Michael Himes, "The 3 Key Questions," YouTube video, https:// www.youtube.com/watch?v=P-4lKCENdnw.

Chapter 9

1. Pope Francis, "Ceremony Commemorating the 50th Anniversary of the Institution of the Synod of Bishops," October 17, 2015, https:// www.vatican.va/content/francesco/en/speeches/2015/october/documents /papa-francesco_20151017_50-anniversario-sinodo.html.

2. Antonio Spadaro, "A Big Heart Open to God: An Interview with Pope Francis," *America*, September 30, 2013, https://www.america magazine.org/faith/2013/09/30/big-heart-open-god-interview-pope -francis.

3. Avery Dulles, *Models of the Church*, exp. ed. (New York: Doubleday, 2002), 50.

4. Dulles, *Models*, 186.

5. Dulles, 79.

6. Dulles, 85.

7. *Lumen Gentium* (November 21, 1964), 8, in Austin Flannery, ed., *Vatican Council II: Constitutions, Decrees, Declarations; The Basic Sixteen Documents* (Collegeville, MN: Liturgical Press, 2014).

8. Francis, "50th Anniversary."

9. Francis, "50th Anniversary."